Two-Hour Nature Crafts

Two-Hour Nature Crafts

McKenzie Kate

Sterling Publishing Co., Inc. New York
A Sterling / Chapelle Book

Chapelle:
- Jo Packham, Owner
- Cathy Sexton, Editor
- Karmen Quinney, Assistant to Editor
- Staff: Malissa Boatwright, Kass Burchett, Rebecca Christensen, Marilyn Goff, Michael Hannah, Amber Hansen, Shirley Heslop, Holly Hollingsworth, Susan Jorgensen, Barbara Milburn, Leslie Ridenour, and Cindy Stoeckl

McKenzie Kate Designers:
- Rebecca Carter
- Debbie Crabtree-Lewis
- Emily Dinsdale
- Kathy Distefano-Griffiths

Fresh Floral Arrangement Designers:
- Susan Laws
- Cindy Rooks

Photography:
- Kevin Dilley, Photographer for Hazen Photography
- Susan Laws, Jo Packham, and Cindy Rooks, Photo Stylists for Chapelle

- A special thanks to Nature's Pressed and Mountains to Meadows, both of Orem, Utah, for their donations of the pressed flowers and greenery and natural soaps used in this publication.

If you have any questions or comments or would like information on specialty products featured in this book, please contact Chapelle, Ltd., Inc., P.O. Box 9252, Ogden, UT 84409 • (801) 621-2777 • (801) 621-2788 Fax

Library of Congress Cataloging-in-Publication Data

Kate, McKenzie.
     Two-hour nature crafts / McKenzie Kate.
              p.   cm.
     "A Sterling / Chapelle book."
     Includes index.
     ISBN 0-8069-4293-2
     1. Nature craft.   I. Title.
TT157.K355 1997
745.5--dc20   96-38702
                                                                  CIP

10 9 8 7 6 5 4 3 2 1

Published by Sterling Publishing Company, Inc.
387 Park Avenue South, New York, NY 10016
© 1997 by Chapelle Ltd.
Distributed in Canada by Sterling Publishing
c/o Canadian Manda Group, One Atlantic Avenue, Suite 105
Toronto, Ontario, Canada M6K 3E7
Distributed in Great Britain and Europe by Cassell PLC
Wellington House, 125 Strand, London WC2R 0BB, England
Distributed in Australia by Capricorn Link (Australia) Pty Ltd.
P.O. Box 6651, Baulkham Hills, Business Centre, NSW 2153, Australia
Printed and Bound in Hong Kong
All Rights Reserved

Sterling ISBN 0-8069-4293-2

Contents ...

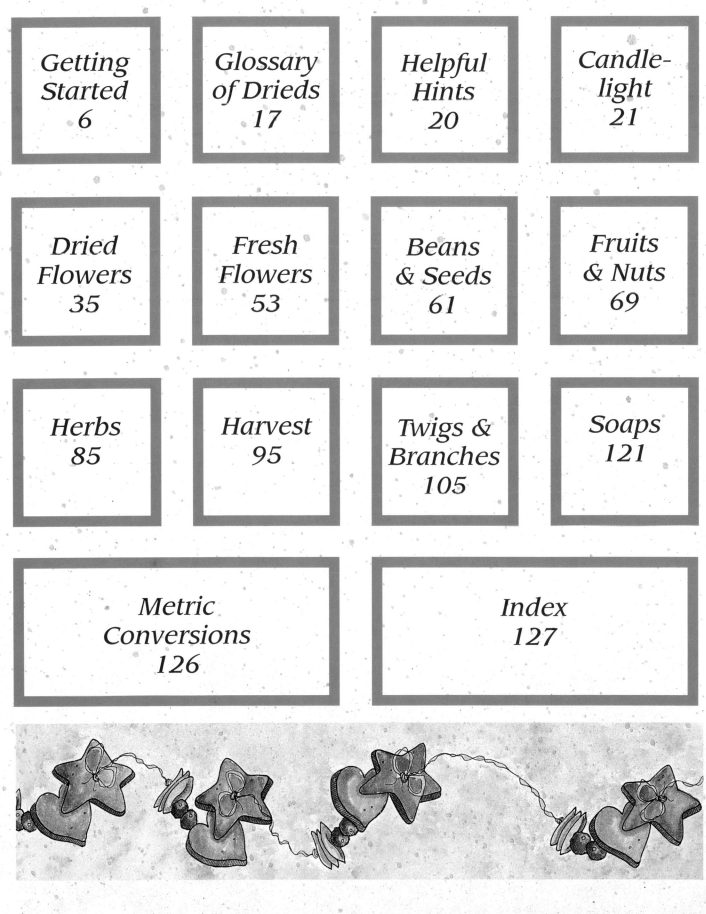

Getting Started ...

Air Drying Long-Stemmed Flowers & Leaves

Materials

- ❧ Bundles of fresh flowers & leaves
- ❧ String or rubberbands
- ❧ Spare room, garage, or shed

Instructions

1. Gather six to ten stems and tie string around ends (or use rubberband) to secure bundle.

2. Hang bundles upside-down in a spare room, garage, or shed. Make certain the bundles are hung in a dry environment, preferably out of the sun to avoid bleaching.

3. Allow to dry thoroughly.

Air Drying Short-Stemmed Flowers & Leaves

Materials

- ❧ Loose fresh flowers & leaves
- ❧ Window screen
- ❧ Bricks (4)
- ❧ Spare room, garage, or shed

Instructions

1. Place window screen up on four bricks in a spare room, garage, or shed. Make certain the window screen is placed in a dry environment, preferably out of the sun to avoid bleaching.

2. Place loose flowers and leaves on top of window screen without overlapping.

3. Allow to dry thoroughly.

Drying Flowers & Leaves Slowly with Silica Gel

Materials

- Loose fresh flowers & leaves
- Silica gel
- Container, metal, glass, or plastic
- Paintbrush, soft

Instructions

1. Place one inch of silica gel (moisture-absorbent crystals) into container.

2. Place loose flowers and leaves on top of silica gel without overlapping.

3. Cover loose flowers and leaves with a thin layer of silica gel just until flowers and leaves are covered.

4. Repeat process until container is full.

5. Allow to dry thoroughly; check every other day.

6. Using a soft paintbrush, whisk away any lingering silica gel crystals.

Drying Flowers & Leaves Quickly with Silica Gel

Materials

- Loose fresh flowers & leaves
- Silica gel
- Container, microwave-safe
- Microwave oven
- Paintbrush, soft

Instructions

1. Place one inch of silica gel into container.

2. Place loose flowers and leaves on top of silica gel without overlapping.

3. Cover loose flowers and leaves with a thin layer of silica gel just until flowers and leaves are covered.

4. Place container in microwave oven and heat on medium for one to two minutes.

5. Remove and allow to stand for 30 minutes.

6. Using a soft paintbrush, whisk away any lingering silica gel crystals.

Pressing Flowers & Leaves

Materials

- Loose fresh flowers & leaves
- Plywood: $1/4$"-thick squares (2)
- Cardboard, corrugated
- Watercolor paper or absorbent paper
- Acrylic paints
- Tweezers
- Toothpick
- Craft glue
- Découpage glue, optional
- Paintbrush
- Flat screws, $1^{1}/2$" (4)
- Wing nuts (4)
- Drill with $1/8$" drill bit
- Scissors

Instructions for Making Flower Presses

1. Each flower press consists of two plywood squares, four flat screws, and four wing nuts. Note: The size of the flower press (the plywood squares) is determined by the size of the flowers or leaves to be pressed.

2. Drill one hole in each corner of each plywood square with drill and $1/8$" drill bit.

3. Using a paintbrush, paint plywood squares with acrylic paints as desired.

4. If desired, embellish one side of each plywood square with pressed flowers and leaves by gluing them on and then applying découpage glue over the top according to manufacturer's directions.

Instructions for Pressing Flowers & Leaves

1. Cut cardboard and watercolor paper into circles with scissors, using the size of the plywood squares to determine the diameter of the circles. Note: Cut several of each.

2. Begin by placing one plywood square on working surface. Next, place one cardboard circle on top of plywood square. Next, place one watercolor paper circle on top of cardboard. Next, place fresh flower or leaf to be pressed.

3. Place another watercolor paper circle on top of fresh flower or leaf, followed by another cardboard circle.

4. Repeat process until flowers and leaves are each between watercolor paper and cardboard circles. Note: Keep the flower press to a stacked height of about one inch or less.

5. Place the remaining plywood square on top of last cardboard circle.

6. Holding flower press together firmly, place flat screw into drilled hole in each corner.

7. Place wing nuts on flat screws and tighten until flower press appears tight enough that flowers and leaves are being pressed adequately.

8. Allow to press for seven to ten days.

9. Carefully remove pressed flowers and leaves from between watercolor circles.

Making Wreaths

Materials

- ❦ Grapevines
- ❦ Twigs, green
- ❦ Branches, green
- ❦ Copper wire: 19-gauge
- ❦ Floral wire

Instructions for Grapevine Wreaths

1. Soak grapevines in water until pliable.

2. Place grapevines together with ends staggered slightly and bend into desired shape.

3. Hold grapevines in place and wrap the longest grapevine around the shaped grapevines, making certain all grapevines are secured. Tuck in stray ends.

Instructions for Green Twig & Branch Wreaths

1. Bend green twigs or branches into desired shape and secure them with copper or floral wire.

2. Allow wreath to sit in the sun for several days for green twigs or branches to dry thoroughly.

Embellishing Wreaths

Materials

- ❦ Wreath
- ❦ Embellishments
- ❦ Ribbon
- ❦ Floral wire
- ❦ Hot glue gun & glue sticks
- ❦ Scissors

Instructions

1. Choose desired embellishments — dried and fresh flowers and greenery, nuts, and pinecones are a few among many to choose from.

2. Divide embellishments into groups for easy access.

3. Begin by arranging the largest items on the wreath and, using a hot glue gun and glue sticks, hot-glue in place.

4. Repeat process for remaining embellishments, from largest to smallest.

5. Tie ribbon in a bow according to instructions for Making Multi-Loop Bows on page 14.

6. Using hot glue gun and glue sticks, hot-glue bow to wreath or, using floral wire, secure bow in place. Cascade ribbon tails down.

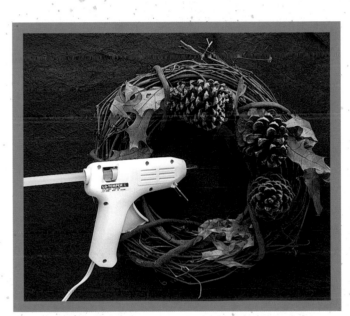

What is Beeswax?

Beeswax is a very pliable, natural substance that is secreted by bees and creates the honeycomb that actually holds the honey.

The honey is extracted by heating the honeycomb until the honey runs free from the honeycomb shell. Then the honeycomb, or beeswax, is cleaned and ready to be used.

The color of beeswax ranges in shades, but always has a dull-yellow or amber coloring.

What is Candle Wax?

Candle wax is wax that has a hardening additive. It melts at a higher temperature than paraffin wax.

The color of candle wax is translucent, but can be changed with candle dyes.

What is Paraffin Wax?

Paraffin wax is a soft wax. It melts at a lower temperature than candle wax.

The color of paraffin wax is translucent, but can be changed with candle dyes.

Generally, paraffin wax is too soft for making decorative candles, but is ideal for re-dipping candles or sealing bottles.

Using Candle Dyes

Candle wax and paraffin wax colors can be changed simply by adding a candle dye. Candle dyes come in several colors and will render a rich and vibrant shade.

Old candles and crayons can be used as candle dyes, however the shade of color will be a tint rather than a deep color.

Using Candle Fragrance Oils

Candle fragrance oils can be purchased and have been specially formulated to be used in candle making. Always refer to manufacturer's directions. _Caution: Never use alcohol- or water-based fragrances for scenting candles, they will cause the hot wax to pop and explode._

Melting Wax

Materials

* Saucepan, double-boiler, or crockpot
* Tin can
* Pliers
* Heat source
* Beeswax, candle wax, or paraffin wax

Instructions

1. Place enough water in saucepan, double-boiler, or crockpot to adequately heat sides of tin can.

2. Place on stove or plug-in heating appliance and heat on low. _Note: Higher temperatures will burn the wax and/or cause the hot wax to pop and explode._

3. Place wax in tin can and place tin can in saucepan, double-boiler, or crockpot. _Note: Do not get water in the wax._

4. Wax will slowly begin to melt. _Caution: If wax begins to smoke it is being melted too quickly at too high a temperature — remove from heat immediately as hot wax will ignite. Note: Melted wax is very difficult to remove from pans, utensils, and clothing. Use old items that can be discarded._

5. When wax is completely melted and ready to use, carefully remove tin can containing melted wax from hot water with pliers. _Caution: The melted wax and the tin can will be very hot and can cause serious burns._

Re-dipping Candles

Materials

- ❦ Saucepan, double-boiler, or crockpot
- ❦ Tin can
- ❦ Pliers
- ❦ Heat source
- ❦ Paraffin wax
- ❦ Salad tongs
- ❦ Waxed paper

Instructions

1. Melt paraffin wax according to instructions for Melting Wax on page 10.

2. Using pliers (or needle-nose pliers), pick up candles by candlewicks. Quickly place candle into tin can containing melted wax until candle has been completely submerged. Note: Dip candles into hot wax only once unless indicated otherwise.

3. Using salad tongs, remove candle from hot wax and place on waxed paper to cool thoroughly.

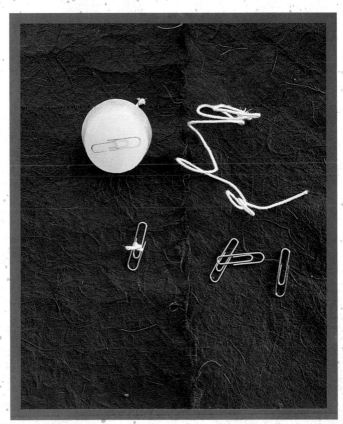

Making & Using Candlewicks

Materials

- ❦ Borax: 2 tablespoons
- ❦ Salt: 1 tablespoon
- ❦ Water: 1 cup
- ❦ Container
- ❦ Cord, cotton
- ❦ Candle mold
- ❦ Paper clips
- ❦ Scissors

Instructions

1. Place Borax, salt, and water in container and soak cord overnight.

2. Remove cord from solution and allow cord to dry thoroughly.

3. Cut candlewick to desired length with scissors.

4. Insert candlewick through a paper clip and fold lengthwise. Twist ends together.

5. Place paper clip in bottom of candle mold.

6. Pour hot wax into candle mold and hold onto end of candlewick until the wax sets enough that candlewick cannot sink back into the wax.

Making Bird Nests

Materials

- Spanish moss
- Leaves, dried
- Twigs
- Acrylic spray, matte
- Adhesive spray

Instructions

1. The amount of Spanish moss needed depends on the desired size of bird nest.

2. Form bird nest by hollowing out center of Spanish moss, pushing excess out toward the sides.

3. Spray bird nest with adhesive spray and slightly press Spanish moss so it adheres to itself.

4. Randomly add dried leaves and twigs.

5. Allow adhesive spray to dry thoroughly.

6. To seal bird nest, spray with matte acrylic spray.

7. Allow acrylic spray to dry thoroughly.

Making Wasp Nests

Materials

- Styrofoam egg: small
- Toilet paper, white
- Acrylic paints: Dark gray Light gray
- Paintbrush
- Spray bottle
- Craft knife
- Pencil

Instructions

1. Cut $^1/_4$" off pointed end of styrofoam egg with craft knife.

2. Make a $^1/_2$" deep hole in flat end of styrofoam egg with a pencil.

3. Tear toilet paper sheets into three or four strips. Wet strips with spray bottle and wrap around and inside hole in styrofoam egg, allowing a few strips to pull away from sides of styrofoam egg.

4. Allow toilet paper to dry thoroughly.

5. Using a paint-brush, make rings around styrofoam egg with dark gray acrylic paint.

6. Repeat process with light gray acrylic paint, blending paints as desired.

7. Allow paint to dry thoroughly after each step.

Painting Wooden Eggs

Materials

- Wooden eggs
- Acrylic paints:
    Black
    Cream
    Gold
    Sandstone
- Paintbrush
- Toothbrush
- Foam plate
- Acrylic spray, gloss

Instructions

1. Place a small dab of each acrylic paint color on a foam plate.

2. Using a paintbrush, load bristles with cream and sandstone acrylic paints.

3. Using up and down strokes, paint wooden eggs.

4. Allow paint to dry thoroughly.

5. Using a paintbrush, load bristles with gold.

6. Streak paint on eggs making certain gold does not stand out. <u>Note: Colors should blend, yet show through individually.</u>

7. Allow paint to dry thoroughly.

8. Lightly dip toothbrush in black. Hold toothbrush six inches from eggs and spatter by running a finger up the toothbrush bristles.

9. Allow paint to dry thoroughly.

10. To seal wooden eggs, spray with gloss acrylic spray.

11. Allow acrylic spray to dry thoroughly.

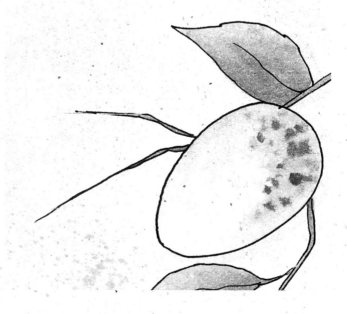

Making Natural Soap

Materials

- ❦ Water: 1¼ cups
- ❦ Lye: 4 tablespoons
- ❦ Coconut oil: 3 tablespoons
- ❦ Sunflower oil: 3½ tablespoons
- ❦ Olive oil: 3 tablespoons
- ❦ Herbal oil: 1½ teaspoons
- ❦ Food coloring: 2 drops, optional
- ❦ Oatmeal, fine: 4 tablespoons, optional
- ❦ Honey: 2 tablespoons, optional
- ❦ Glass bowl
- ❦ Saucepan
- ❦ Wooden spoon
- ❦ Wire whisk
- ❦ Rubber gloves
- ❦ Newspaper
- ❦ Waxed paper
- ❦ Candle molds or small baking tins

Instructions

1. Working over newspaper, place water in a glass bowl. <u>Note: Do not use a metal bowl; lye will eat the metal.</u>

2. Carefully pour lye into water and stir with a wooden spoon until lye dissolves. Set aside. <u>Caution: Lye is an alkali that can cause serious burns. Rubber gloves should be worn at all times when working with lye. If lye should come into contact with the skin, immediately wash affected areas with cold water. Vinegar or lemon juice will help ease the pain from the burn.</u>

3. Place oils in a saucepan and heat on low until oil is lukewarm.

4. Pour lukewarm oil into glass bowl containing lye mixture, stirring constantly.

5. If desired, add food coloring. Beat together with wire whisk until thick.

6. Pour mixture into candle molds or baking tins and set aside for 24 hours.

7. Remove soap from candle molds or baking tins and wrap in waxed paper.

8. Store in a cool place for three weeks to allow soap to harden thoroughly.

9. If desired, add oatmeal and honey to lye mixture to make natural oatmeal soap.

Glossary of Drieds ...

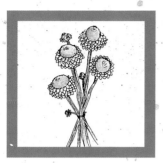

Ammobium
(Ammobium
alatum)

Calendula
(Calendula
officinalis)

Caspia
(Miniature
Statice)

Cedar Rose
(Deodara
rosa)

Cedar Tips
(Deodara)

Cockscomb
(Celosia
argentea)

Corn Flowers
(Centaurea
montana)

Deer Moss
(Cladonia
rangiferina)

Eucalyptus
(Eucalyptus
gunnii)

Fern
(Plumosa)

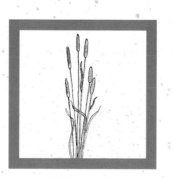

Foxtail Millet
(Panicum
miliaceum)

Galoxa Leaf
(Galeax)

Garlic Bulb
(Allium
sativum)

German Statice
(Limonium
globus)

Globe
Amaranth

Heather
(Calluna
vulgaris)

Juniper Berries
(Juniperus
sabina)

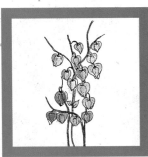

Lantern
Pods

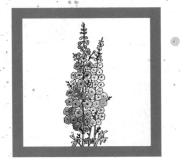

Larkspur
(Consolida
ambigua)

Lavender
(Lavendula
angustifolia)

Lemon Leaf
(Citrus
limonium)

Licopodium
or Princess Pine

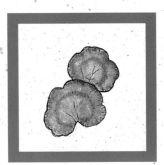

Mushrooms
(Trametes
vericolor)

Myrtle Leaf
(Myrtus
communis)

Nigella or
Love in a Mist

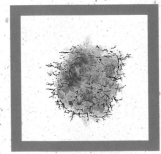

Oregon Moss
(Sphagnum)

Pepper Berries
(Clelthra
alnifloia)

Pinecones
(Pinus)

Pomegranate
(Punica
granatum)

Poppy Pods
(Papaver
orientale)

Pussy Willows
(Salix
discolor)

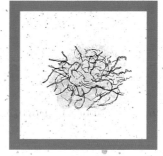

River Birch
Cones
(Betula)

Rosebuds
(Rosa)

Rose hips
(Rosa
gallica)

Safflower
(Carthamus
tinctorius)

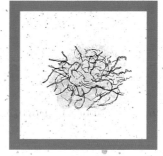

Spanish Moss
(Tillandria
usneoides)

Star Anise
(Pimpinella
anisum)

Statice Sinuata
(Limonium
sinuata)

Straw Flowers
(Helichrysum
bracteatum)

Sunflower
Seed Head
(Helianthus
annus)

Sunflowers
(Helianthus)

Wheat Stem
(Triticum)

Wild Grass
(Gramineae)

Yarrow
(Achillea
millefolium)

19

Helpful Hints ...

❦ When making dried floral arrangements, use styrofoam or floral foam that has been made for drieds. Foam that has been made for fresh floral arrangements will not work because it deteriorates easily and will not hold drieds permanently.

❦ When using deer moss, Oregon moss, or Spanish moss in dried floral arrangements, soak the moss in a bucket of water. This will make the moss soft and pliable and eliminate airborne particles.

❦ When using deer moss, Oregon moss, or Spanish moss in dried floral arrangements, allow some wisps of moss to show through for an enhanced look of nature.

❦ Garlic bulbs maintain their freshness for about three months. Once the garlic bulbs begin to turn lavender in color, it is time for them to be used. Simply remove the garlic bulbs from the dried arrangement and replace them with fresh ones.

❦ When using fresh fruits, dip them in lemon juice before drying to prevent the fruit from darkening in color.

❦ Before drying fragile flowers, greenery, grasses, grains, and pods, spray with a fixative such as hair spray to seal surfaces.

❦ When working with fresh flowers, cut stems at an angle with sharp scissors and immediately place in a bucket of cool water for several hours before using.

❦ When displaying fresh flowers, an aspirin added to the flower vase can prolong the life of the fresh flowers. It is recommended that the water in the flower vase be changed and another aspirin added every one or two days.

❦ Embellished candles are best used for decorative purposes only.

❦ Never allow a candle to burn lower than three inches of display height and never leave a candle unattended.

❦ After time, dried flowers begin to look dull and unnatural. When this happens, try steaming the dried flowers back to life.

❦ Small bird nests make fun decorative accessories. Place them on top of drapery rods, along window sills, and on top of doorways.

❦ Do not display potpourri on window sills as direct sunlight fades its color.

❦ When displaying potpourri, always keep out of reach of children and pets.

Candlelight ...

Pinecone Firestarters

Materials

- ❧ Pinecones
- ❧ Candle wax
- ❧ Candle dyes, optional
- ❧ Candle fragrance oils, optional
- ❧ Saucepan
- ❧ Tin can
- ❧ Pliers
- ❧ Salad tongs
- ❧ Waxed paper

Instructions

1. Melt wax according to instructions for Melting Wax on page 10. If desired, add candle dyes and fragrance oils.

2. Using salad tongs, dip pinecones upside-down into hot wax. Dip each pinecone twice.

3. Remove pinecones from hot wax and place on waxed paper to cool thoroughly.

4. A pine scent will enhance the aroma once the pinecones begin to burn. _Caution: If the pinecones are extremely dry, they will pop and crackle while they burn and will likely send out sparks._

Santa Sticks

Materials

- ❧ Cinnamon sticks
- ❧ Acrylic paints:
     Black
     Caucasian flesh
     Red
     White
- ❧ Paintbrush
- ❧ Raffia
- ❧ Straight pin

Instructions

1. Using a paintbrush, paint ¹/₂" of one end of each cinnamon stick with Caucasian flesh acrylic paint for Santa's face.

2. Paint Santa's beard and hair with white.

3. Paint end of cinnamon stick with red for Santa's hat.

4. Using the head of a straight pin, dot Santa's eyes with black. Dot Santa's nose and cheeks with red. Dot a pompon on Santa's hat with white.

5. Allow paint to dry thoroughly after each step.

6. Repeat process for each cinnamon stick.

7. Gather Santa Sticks and tie raffia around center to secure bundle.

Pinecone Cupcake Firestarters

Materials

- ❧ Pinecones
- ❧ Candle wax
- ❧ Candle dyes, optional
- ❧ Candle fragrance oils, optional
- ❧ Embellishments, as desired
- ❧ Cupcake tin, non-stick
- ❧ Saucepan
- ❧ Tin can
- ❧ Pliers
- ❧ Salad tongs
- ❧ Waxed paper

Instructions

1. Melt wax according to instructions for Melting Wax on page 10. If desired, add candle dyes and fragrance oils.

2. Pour hot wax into cupcake tin, ²/₃ full.

3. Place one pinecone, facing up, in the center of each "cupcake" and push down into hot wax.

4. Place cupcake tin in refrigerator to cool for about one hour.

5. Remove cupcake tin from refrigerator and place in a cold water bath. This helps loosen wax around edges.

6. One at a time, pick up each "cupcake" by the bottom with salad tongs. Dip pinecones upside-down into hot wax. Dip each pinecone twice.

7. Remove pinecones from hot wax and place on waxed paper to cool thoroughly.

8. Embellish pinecone cupcakes as desired.

Molded Beehive Candle

Materials

- Beehive with bees candle mold
- Beeswax
- Candlewick
- Saucepan
- Tin can
- Pliers
- Waxed paper

Instructions

1. Melt wax according to instructions for Melting Wax on page 10.

2. Place candlewick in bottom of candle mold. Home-made candlewicks can be made according to instructions for Making & Using Candlewicks on page 11.

3. Pour hot wax into candle mold and hold onto end of candlewick until the wax sets enough that candlewick cannot sink back into the wax.

4. Allow wax to cool for about 15 minutes before removing candle from candle mold.

5. Remove candle from candle mold and place on waxed paper to cool thoroughly.

Pressed Flower Candle

Materials

- Candle: any size
- Pressed flowers
- Pressed greenery
- Tweezers
- Toothpick
- Craft glue
- Découpage glue
- Paintbrush

Instructions

1. Using tweezers, pick up pressed flowers and greenery.

2. Using a toothpick, apply craft glue to back sides of pressed flowers and greenery.

3. Carefully arrange pressed flowers and greenery on front of candle.

4. Allow glue to dry thoroughly.

5. Using a paintbrush, apply découpage glue over pressed flowers and greenery on front of candle according to manufacturer's directions.

Re-dipped Flower Candles

Materials

- ❧ Candles: any size
- ❧ Pressed flowers
- ❧ Pressed greenery
- ❧ Raffia, optional
- ❧ Tweezers
- ❧ Toothpick
- ❧ Craft glue
- ❧ Paraffin wax
- ❧ Saucepan
- ❧ Tin can
- ❧ Pliers
- ❧ Salad tongs
- ❧ Waxed paper

Instructions

1. Using tweezers, pick up pressed flowers and greenery.

2. Using a toothpick, apply craft glue to back sides of pressed flowers and greenery.

3. Carefully arrange pressed flowers and greenery on front of candles.

4. Allow glue to dry thoroughly.

5. Melt wax according to instructions for Melting Wax on page 10.

6. Dip embellished candles into hot wax according to instructions for Re-dipping Candles on page 11.

7. Using salad tongs, remove candles from hot wax and place on waxed paper to cool thoroughly.

8. If desired, tie raffia around candles and tie raffia in bows.

Re-dipped Cinnamon Candle

Materials

- ❦ Candle: any size
- ❦ Cinnamon sticks
- ❦ Raffia
- ❦ Toothpick
- ❦ Craft glue
- ❦ Paraffin wax
- ❦ Saucepan
- ❦ Tin can
- ❦ Pliers
- ❦ Salad tongs
- ❦ Waxed paper
- ❦ Scissors

Instructions

1. Break cinnamon sticks into uniform lengths.

2. Using a toothpick, apply craft glue to back sides of cinnamon sticks.

3. Carefully arrange cinnamon sticks around candle.

4. Allow glue to dry thoroughly.

5. Tie raffia around candle to secure cinnamon sticks.

6. Melt wax according to instructions for Melting Wax on page 10.

7. Dip embellished candle into hot wax according to instructions for Re-dipping Candles on page 11.

8. Using salad tongs, remove candle from hot wax and place on waxed paper to cool thoroughly.

9. Tie more raffia around candle.

10. Trim ends of raffia with scissors.

Re-dipped Bay Leaf Candle

Materials

- Candle: any size
- Bay leaves, dried
- Raffia
- Toothpick
- Craft glue
- Paraffin wax
- Saucepan
- Tin can
- Pliers
- Salad tongs
- Waxed paper
- Scissors

Instructions

1. Using a toothpick, apply craft glue to back sides of bay leaves.

2. Carefully arrange bay leaves around candle.

3. Allow glue to dry thoroughly.

4. Tie raffia around candle to secure bay leaves.

5. Melt wax according to instructions for Melting Wax on page 10.

6. Dip embellished candle into hot wax according to instructions for Re-dipping Candles on page 11.

7. Using salad tongs, remove candle from hot wax and place on waxed paper to cool thoroughly.

8. Tie more raffia around candle.

9. Trim ends of raffia with scissors.

Log Candles

Materials

- ❧ Logs: any size
- ❧ Candle wax
- ❧ Candle dyes, optional
- ❧ Candle fragrance oils, optional
- ❧ Candlewicks
- ❧ Raffia or jute
- ❧ Saucepan
- ❧ Tin can
- ❧ Pliers
- ❧ Drill with 3" forstner bit

Instructions

1. Drill 3"-diameter holes in tops of logs with drill and forstner bit. The holes can be any depth desired, but it is recommended that the bottom 2" of logs remain undrilled. Note: A forstner bit is a wide drill bit that makes a flat bottom if not allowed to penetrate through the entire log or piece of wood.

2. Melt wax according to instructions for Melting Wax on page 10. If desired, add candle dyes and fragrance oils.

3. Place candlewick in bottom of each drilled hole. Homemade candlewicks can be made according to instructions for Making & Using Candlewicks on page 11.

4. One at a time, pour hot wax into drilled hole of each log. Hold onto end of candlewick until the wax sets enough that candlewick cannot sink back into the wax.

5. Allow wax to cool thoroughly.

6. Tie raffia or jute around logs.

7. Tie raffia or jute in a bow.

Spiced Ornament Candle

Materials

- ❦ Candle: any size
- ❦ Ground cinnamon: 1 cup
- ❦ Ground cloves: 1 tablespoon
- ❦ Ground nutmeg: 1 tablespoon
- ❦ Applesauce: 3/4 cup
- ❦ All-purpose glue: 2 tablespoons
- ❦ Water: 3/4 to 1 cup
- ❦ Jute, waxed
- ❦ Toothpick
- ❦ Cookie cutter, heart-shaped
- ❦ Mixing bowl
- ❦ Wooden spoon
- ❦ Cookie sheet

Instructions

1. Make heart-shaped spiced ornaments according to instructions for Making Spiced Ornaments on page 15.

2. String heart-shaped spiced ornaments onto jute so they hang nicely.

3. Tie jute around candle.

Cinnamon & Jute Candle

Materials

- ❦ Candle: any size
- ❦ Cinnamon sticks
- ❦ Jute: 2-ply & 3-ply
- ❦ Craft glue

Instructions

1. Tie 2-ply jute around candle and tie knots at each end.

2. Break cinnamon sticks into various lengths.

3. Apply craft glue to cinnamon sticks and glue to 2-ply jute all the way around candle.

4. Allow glue to dry thoroughly.

5. Tie 3-ply jute around candle to secure cinnamon sticks.

6. Tie 3-ply jute in a bow and tie knots at each end.

Cupcake Candles

Materials

- ❦ Cedar chips
- ❦ Potpourri
- ❦ Rosebuds & rose petals, dried
- ❦ Orange slices, dried
- ❦ Candle wax
- ❦ Candle dyes, optional
- ❦ Candle fragrance oils, optional
- ❦ Candlewicks
- ❦ Cupcake tin, non-stick
- ❦ Saucepan
- ❦ Tin can
- ❦ Pliers
- ❦ Waxed paper

Instructions

1. Melt wax according to instructions for Melting Wax on page 10. If desired, add candle dyes and fragrance oils.

2. Fill cupcake tin $^1/_3$ full with cedar chips, potpourri, rosebuds and rose petals, or orange slices.

3. Place candle-wick in bottom of each "cupcake." Homemade candle-wicks can be made according to instructions for Making & Using Candlewicks on page 11.

4. Pour hot wax into cupcake tin until full. Hold onto end of each candlewick until the wax sets enough that candle-wick cannot sink back into the wax.

5. Place cupcake tin in refrigerator to cool for about one hour.

6. Remove cupcake tin from refrigerator and place in a cold water bath. This helps loosen wax around edges.

7. Carefully remove candles from cupcake tin.

8. Cupcake candles are generally used as firestarters. See Pinecone Cupcake Firestarters on page 23.

Woodland Candle Box

Materials

- ❦ Candle: 8" high
- ❦ Papier-mâché box with lid, hexagon: 6"-diameter
- ❦ Styrofoam block: 4"-square x 3"-thick
- ❦ Oregon moss
- ❦ Pomegranate, dried
- ❦ Poppy pods, dried
- ❦ Nuts, assorted
- ❦ Pinecones
- ❦ Cinnamon sticks: 12"-long (8)
- ❦ Grapevine wreath: 3"-diameter
- ❦ Jute: 3-ply
- ❦ Spray stain, green
- ❦ Craft glue

Instructions

1. Spray papier-mâché box and lid with spray stain.

2. Allow spray stain to dry thoroughly.

3. Place lid on bottom of box.

4. Tie jute around sides of box and lid to secure lid to box.

5. Apply craft glue to bottom of candle and glue into one corner of box.

6. Apply craft glue to bottom of styrofoam block and glue into box next to candle.

7. Allow glue to dry thoroughly.

8. Apply craft glue to top and sides of styrofoam block and glue Oregon moss around it.

9. Apply craft glue to the pomegranate, poppy pods, nuts, pinecones, and cinnamon sticks.

10. Carefully arrange the pomegranate, poppy pods, nuts, pinecones, and cinnamon sticks on styrofoam block and inside box around candle.

11. Apply craft glue to grapevine wreath and glue into box next to candle.

12. Allow glue to dry thoroughly.

13. Tie three jute bows and randomly tie knots in tails.

14. Using craft glue, glue bows into center of arrangement.

15. Allow glue to dry thoroughly.

Berries & Pinecone Candle

Materials

- ❧ Candle: any size
- ❧ Log slab
- ❧ Berries, dried
- ❧ Nuts, assorted
- ❧ Pinecones
- ❧ Jute: 2-ply
- ❧ Wooden candle cup: to fit diameter of candle
- ❧ Hot glue gun & glue sticks
- ❧ Wood glue

Instructions

1. Using wood glue, adhere wooden candle cup to top of log slab, centered.

2. Allow glue to dry thoroughly.

3. Carefully arrange berries, nuts, and pinecones around wooden candle cup.

4. Using hot glue gun and glue sticks, hot-glue berries, nuts, and pinecones in place.

5. Tie jute around log slab.

6. Tie jute in a bow and randomly tie two knots at each end.

7. Carefully place candle in wooden candle cup.

Dried Flower Lamp

Materials

- ❦ Decorative bottle
- ❦ Globe amaranth, dried
- ❦ Rosebuds, dried
- ❦ Statice sinuata
- ❦ Pepper berries, dried
- ❦ Fern, dried
- ❦ Pearl beads
- ❦ Porcelain drawer pull: to fit bottle opening
- ❦ Candlewick
- ❦ Glass wick
- ❦ Lamp oil

Instructions

1. Fill decorative bottle with globe amaranth, rosebuds, statice sinuata, pepper berries, fern, and pearl beads.

2. Turn bottle up-side-down and gently shake to remove broken pieces from dried flowers.

3. Fill bottle with lamp oil.

4. Place candlewick inside glass wick. Place glass wick inside hole in porcelain drawer pull.

5. Place drawer pull in opening of bottle.

33

Gift Candles

Materials

- ❧ Tapered candles: 12" (2)
- ❧ Orange slices, dried
- ❧ Straw flowers
- ❧ Raffia
- ❧ Tissue paper
- ❧ Cardboard: 3" x 14"
- ❧ Craft glue

Instructions

1. Tear edges of tissue paper.

2. One at a time, roll centers of candles in tissue paper.

3. Place wrapped candles on cardboard.

4. Apply craft glue to orange slices and straw flowers.

5. Carefully arrange orange slices and straw flowers on front of wrapped candles.

6. Allow glue to dry thoroughly.

7. Tie raffia around cardboard, candles, and orange slices.

8. Tie raffia in a bow.

Dried Flowers ...

Dried Sunflower Basket

Photograph on page 35.

Materials

- ❧ Decorative basket
- ❧ Sunflowers, dried
- ❧ Yarrow, dried
- ❧ Larkspur, dried
- ❧ Nigella, dried
- ❧ Poppy pods, dried
- ❧ Eucalyptus, silver dollar
- ❧ Lemon leaves, dried
- ❧ Spanish moss
- ❧ Raffia
- ❧ Floral foam for drieds, to fit inside basket
- ❧ Floral pins
- ❧ Copper wire: 19-gauge
- ❧ Watering can, tin: miniature
- ❧ Hot glue gun & glue sticks

Instructions

1. Place floral foam inside basket, making certain it fits tightly all the way around the edges.

2. Using floral pins, cover floral foam with Spanish moss until it is completely covered.

3. Beginning with the largest flowers, carefully arrange sunflowers, yarrow, larkspur, nigella, poppy pods, eucalyptus, and lemon leaves in basket in a triangular shape. Push dried flowers and greenery into floral foam. Make certain the arrangement is even on both sides.

4. Tie raffia in a bow.

5. Using hot glue gun and glue sticks, hot-glue bow to side of basket.

6. Form a copper wire loop and thread it through handle of watering can.

7. Twist copper wire at top to secure, leaving a two-inch long tail.

8. Push copper wire tail into floral foam, hanging watering can on top of raffia bow.

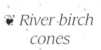

Christmas Corsage

Materials

- ❧ Pine garland: 8" length
- ❧ Licopodium
- ❧ Globe amaranth, dried
- ❧ Cockscomb, dried
- ❧ River birch cones
- ❧ Hot glue gun & glue sticks
- ❧ Corsage pin

Instructions

1. Using pine garland, form a tight circle. Twist tightly to make a base for the corsage.

2. Using hot glue gun and glue sticks, hot-glue licopodium to pine garland base.

3. Carefully arrange and hot-glue cockscomb, globe amaranth, and river birch cones on top of licopodium.

4. Pin to garment with a corsage pin.

Kissing Ball

Materials

- ❦ Globe amaranth, dried
- ❦ Nigella, dried
- ❦ Safflowers, dried
- ❦ Cedar roses
- ❦ Oregon moss
- ❦ Styrofoam ball: 3"-diameter
- ❦ Wired ribbon, 1"-wide, purple
- ❦ Floral wire
- ❦ Corsage pin
- ❦ Craft glue
- ❦ Hot glue gun & glue sticks
- ❦ Scissors

Instructions

1. Apply craft glue to styrofoam ball and glue Oregon moss around it until it is completely covered.

2. Allow glue to dry thoroughly.

3. Tie wired ribbon in a bow according to instructions for Making Multi-Loop Bows on page 14.

4. Using hot glue gun and glue sticks, hot-glue bow to top of styrofoam ball. Cascade ribbon tails over styrofoam ball and hot-glue in place.

5. Carefully arrange and hot-glue globe amaranth, nigella, safflowers, and cedar roses, evenly, around styrofoam ball on top of Oregon moss.

6. Cut wired ribbon into one 12" length with scissors. Fold wired ribbon in half. Tie loose ends of wired ribbon in a knot. Attach knotted end to center top of styrofoam ball with a corsage pin to make a loop for hanging.

Fantasy Ball

Materials

- ❦ Rosebuds, dried
- ❦ Straw flowers
- ❦ Eucalyptus (4)
- ❦ Statice sinuata
- ❦ Pepper berries, dried
- ❦ Pinecones
- ❦ Styrofoam ball: 12½"-diameter
- ❦ Paper ribbon, 3"-wide, tan
- ❦ Wired ribbon, ⅝"-wide, pink iridescent
- ❦ Floral wire
- ❦ Corsage pin
- ❦ Découpage glue
- ❦ Paintbrush
- ❦ Hot glue gun & glue sticks
- ❦ Scissors

Instructions

1. Unravel paper ribbon. Cut into three 12½" lengths with scissors.

2. Cut wired ribbon into two 42" lengths and one 12" length with scissors.

3. Cut eucalyptus into one 10" length and three 6" lengths with scissors.

4. Beginning and ending at the center, wrap one 12½" length of paper ribbon around

styrofoam ball. Repeat process for two remaining 12½" lengths of paper ribbon, over-lapping previous ribbon and com-pletely covering styrofoam ball.

5. Using a paint-brush, apply décou-page glue over paper ribbon according to manufacturer's directions.

6. Unravel more paper ribbon and tie in a bow according to instructions for Making Multi-Loop Bows on page 14.

7. Using hot glue gun and glue sticks, hot-glue bow to top of styrofoam ball. Cascade ribbon tails over styrofoam ball and hot-glue in place.

8. Hot-glue 10" length of eucalyptus to top center of styrofoam ball so it hangs freely and curves down one side. Hot-glue all three 6" lengths of eucalyptus, evenly, to top center of styrofoam ball.

9. Carefully arrange and hot-glue straw flowers, statice sinuata, and pepper berries to styrofoam ball as desired.

10. Tie wired ribbon in two bows accord-ing to instructions for Making Multi-Loop Bows on page 14. Form ten 1½" loops from each 42" length of wired ribbon, leaving six-inch tails, and secure with floral wire.

11. Using hot glue gun and glue sticks, hot-glue one bow to each side of paper ribbon bow. Cascade ribbon tails down and hot-glue in place.

12. Hot-glue one rosebud and one pinecone into center of paper ribbon bow.

13. Carefully arrange and hot-glue remaining rosebuds and pine-cones to styrofoam ball as desired.

14. Fold 12" length of wired ribbon in half. Attach center to top of styrofoam ball with a corsage pin. Tie loose ends of wired ribbon in a knot, leaving two-inch tails, to make a loop for hanging.

Dried Pansy Lampshade

Materials

- ❧ Pansies, dried
- ❧ Spray paint, lavender
- ❧ Tweezers
- ❧ Toothpick
- ❧ Craft glue
- ❧ Lamp with lampshade

Instructions

1. Dry pansies according to instructions for Drying Flowers and Leaves with Silica Gel on page 7.

2. Lightly spray lampshade with lavender spray paint.

3. Allow spray paint to dry thoroughly.

4. Using tweezers, pick up pansies.

5. Using a toothpick, apply craft glue to back sides of pansies.

6. Carefully arrange pansies around lampshade, overlapping petals as desired.

7. Allow glue to dry thoroughly.

Dried Wreath of Many Colors

Materials

- ❧ Grapevine wreath
- ❧ Eucalyptus
- ❧ Yarrow, dried
- ❧ Ammobium, dried
- ❧ Larkspur, dried
- ❧ Lantern pods, dried
- ❧ Straw flowers
- ❧ Caspia
- ❧ German statice
- ❧ Statice sinuata
- ❧ Pepper berries, dried
- ❧ Licopodium
- ❧ Fern, dried
- ❧ Raffia
- ❧ Hot glue gun & glue sticks

Instructions

1. Using hot glue gun and glue sticks, hot-glue eucalyptus, evenly, around outer edge of wreath.

2. Carefully arrange and hot-glue yarrow, evenly, around wreath.

3. Tie several raffia bows.

4. Using hot glue gun and glue sticks, hot-glue bows around wreath.

5. Hot-glue ammobium, larkspur, lantern pods, straw flowers, caspia, German statice, statice sinuata, pepper berries, licopodium, and fern around wreath until it is completely covered.

6. Hot-glue several strands of raffia to lower right hand corner of wreath.

Acorn & Pinecone Wreath

Materials

- Grapevine wreath
- Eucalyptus
- Yarrow, dried
- Acorns
- Pinecones
- Lantern pods, dried
- Oak leaves, dried
- Licopodium
- Raffia
- Acrylic spray, gloss
- Hot glue gun & glue sticks

Instructions

1. Using hot glue gun and glue sticks, hot glue eucalyptus, diagonally, around outer edge of wreath.

2. Carefully arrange and hot-glue yarrow, evenly, around wreath.

3. Hot-glue acorns, pinecones, lantern pods, oak leaves, and licopodium around wreath until it is completely covered.

4. Spray wreath with acrylic spray.

5. Allow acrylic spray to dry thoroughly.

6. Tie raffia in a bow.

7. Using hot glue gun and glue sticks, hot-glue bow to lower left hand corner of wreath.

Wooden Chair & Lantern Pods

Materials

- Wooden chair
- Lantern pods, dried
- Statice sinuata
- Deer moss
- Wired ribbon, ³/₄"-wide, lavender iridescent
- Floral wire
- Hot glue gun & glue sticks
- Scissors

Instructions

1. Using hot glue gun and glue sticks, hot-glue deer moss to one side of wooden chair.

2. Carefully arrange and hot-glue lantern pods and statice sinuata on top of deer moss.

3. Tie wired ribbon in a bow according to instructions for Making Multi-Loop Bows on page 14.

4. Using hot glue gun and glue sticks, hot-glue bow to side of wooden chair just below arrangement. Cascade ribbon tails down and hot-glue in place.

Wooden Chair & Rosebuds

Materials

- Wooden chair
- Rosebuds, dried
- Yarrow, dried
- Berries, dried
- Myrtle leaves, dried
- Baby's breath, dried
- Spanish moss
- Wired ribbon, ³/₄"-wide, gold-yellow ombré
- Floral wire
- Hot glue gun & glue sticks
- Scissors

Instructions

1. Using hot glue gun and glue sticks, hot-glue Spanish moss around arch of wooden chair.

2. Carefully arrange and hot-glue rosebuds, yarrow, berries, myrtle leaves, and baby's breath on top of Spanish moss.

3. Tie wired ribbon in two bows according to instructions for Making Multi-Loop Bows on page 14.

4. Using hot glue gun and glue sticks, hot-glue one bow to each side of wooden chair just below arrangement. Cascade ribbon tails down and hot-glue in place.

5. Hot-glue a small bunch of baby's breath into center of each bow.

6. Twist some wired ribbon and randomly hot-glue it to back of chair across arch. Hot-glue two small loops of wired ribbon to front of chair just below rosebuds.

Cherub Holding Drieds

Materials

- Clay cherub
- Dried flowers, assorted
- Raffia, optional
- Hot glue gun & glue sticks

Instructions

1. Using hot glue gun and glue sticks, hot-glue an assortment of dried flowers into cherub's hands.

2. If desired, tie a raffia bow and hot-glue into dried flower arrangement.

German Statice Twig Wreath

Materials

- Twig wreath
- Rosebuds, dried
- Nigella, dried
- Straw flowers
- Fern, dried
- German statice
- Hot glue gun & glue sticks

Instructions

1. Using hot glue gun and glue sticks, hot-glue fern and German statice, evenly, around outer edge of wreath. Leave a small section at top of wreath without fern and German statice.

2. Carefully arrange and hot-glue rose buds, evenly, around wreath.

3. Randomly arrange and hot-glue nigella and straw flowers around wreath.

Cedar Roses Shadow Box

Materials

- Shadow box, house-shaped
- Globe amaranth, dried
- Pinecone
- Rose hips, dried
- Poppy pods, dried
- Cedar roses
- Oregon moss
- Grapevine wreath: 2"-diameter
- Cardboard
- Spray stain, green
- Hot glue gun & glue sticks
- Scissors

Instructions

1. Spray shadow box with spray stain.

2. Allow spray stain to dry thoroughly.

3. Cut cardboard with scissors to fit bottom sections of shadow box.

4. Using hot glue gun and glue sticks, hot-glue cardboard to back of shadow box and hot-glue Oregon moss into each section of shadow box.

5. Carefully arrange and hot-glue globe amaranth, pinecone, rose hips, poppy pods, and cedar roses into shadow box on top of Oregon moss.

6. Hot-glue grapevine wreath to front of shadow box as desired.

Bird's Nest Shadow Box

Materials

- Shadow box, house-shaped
- Spanish moss
- Leaves, dried
- Twigs
- Nigella, dried
- Straw flowers
- Globe amaranth, dried
- Statice sinuata
- Oregon moss
- Cardboard
- Spray stain, walnut
- Acrylic spray, matte
- Adhesive spray
- Hot glue gun & glue sticks
- Scissors

Instructions

1. Make bird's nest according to instructions for Making Bird Nests on page 12.

2. Spray shadow box with spray stain.

3. Allow spray stain to dry thoroughly.

4. Cut cardboard with scissors to fit bottom sections of shadow box.

5. Using hot glue gun and glue sticks, hot-glue cardboard to back of shadow box and hot-glue Oregon moss into each section of shadow box.

6. Carefully arrange and hot-glue nigella, straw flowers, globe amaranth, and statice sinuata into shadow box on top of Oregon moss.

7. Hot-glue bird's nest in top section of shadow box as desired.

House of Dried Flowers

Materials

- ❧ Shadow box, house-shaped
- ❧ Poppy pods, dried
- ❧ Rosebuds, dried
- ❧ Roses, dried
- ❧ Globe amaranth, dried
- ❧ Statice sinuata
- ❧ Pepper berries, dried
- ❧ Oregon moss
- ❧ Deer moss
- ❧ Tree bark
- ❧ Hot glue gun & glue sticks

Instructions

1. Using hot glue gun and glue sticks, hot-glue tree bark to shadow box for roofs.

2. Randomly hot-glue deer moss on sections of roofs.

3. Hot-glue Oregon moss into each section of shadow box.

4. Carefully arrange and hot-glue poppy pods, rosebuds, roses, globe amaranth, statice sinuata, and pepper berries into shadow box on top of Oregon moss.

Rosebud Potpourri

Materials

- ❧ Ammobium, dried:
  1 cup
- ❧ Cedar tips, dried:
  1 cup
- ❧ Corn flowers,
  dried: 2 cups
- ❧ Globe amaranth,
  dried: 1 cup

- ❧ Lavender, dried:
  4 cups
- ❧ Lemon grass,
  dried:
  1 cup crushed
- ❧ Orris root, dried:
  2 tablespoons
- ❧ Pepper berries,
  dried: 1 cup
- ❧ River birch
  cones: 1 cup
- ❧ Rosebuds, dried:
  1 cup

- ❧ Rose hips, dried:
  1 cup
- ❧ Rose petals, dried:
  2 cups crushed
- ❧ Star anise, dried:
  1 cup
- ❧ Fragrance oils:
  lavender,
  1 ounce;
  rose essence,
  1 ounce
- ❧ Container

Instructions

1. Mix all ingredients together in container with hands.

2. As fragrance dissipates, add more fragrance oils to dried mixture.

3. Keep out of direct sunlight as potpourri will fade.

Rosebud Potpourri Birdhouse

Materials

- ❦ Birdhouse on wooden dowel with base
- ❦ Rosebud potpourri
- ❦ Lavender, dried
- ❦ Acrylic paint, pink
- ❦ Paintbrush
- ❦ Wired ribbon, 1"-wide, silver-lavender ombré
- ❦ Floral wire
- ❦ Craft glue
- ❦ Hot glue gun & glue sticks
- ❦ Scissors

Instructions

1. Using a paintbrush, paint birdhouse, wooden dowel, and base with pink acrylic paint.

2. Allow paint to dry thoroughly.

3. Apply craft glue to roof of birdhouse and glue rosebud potpourri on it until it is completely covered. See Rosebud Potpourri on page 47.

4. Apply craft glue to base of birdhouse and glue rosebud potpourri on it until it is completely covered.

5. Allow glue to dry thoroughly.

6. Apply craft glue to front of birdhouse and glue lavender on it until it is completely covered.

7. Allow glue to dry thoroughly.

8. Tie wired ribbon in a bow according to instructions for Making Multi-Loop Bows on page 14.

9. Using hot glue gun and glue sticks, hot-glue bow to top of wooden dowel just below birdhouse. Cascade ribbon tails down each side.

Rosebud Bird's Nest

Materials

- ❧ Spanish moss
- ❧ Leaves, dried
- ❧ Twigs
- ❧ Oregon moss
- ❧ Rosebuds, dried
- ❧ Caspia
- ❧ Wired ribbon, ³/₄"-wide, lavender iridescent
- ❧ Floral wire
- ❧ Acrylic spray, matte
- ❧ Adhesive spray
- ❧ Craft glue
- ❧ Hot glue gun & glue sticks
- ❧ Scissors

Instructions

1. Make bird's nest according to instructions for Making Bird Nests on page 12.

2. Using three twigs, form a teardrop. Wire at top with floral wire to secure.

3. Apply craft glue to top of teardrop and glue Oregon moss on it.

4. Apply craft glue to bottom of bird's nest and glue to bottom of teardrop.

5. Allow glue to dry thoroughly.

6. Using hot glue gun and glue sticks, hot-glue rosebuds and caspia on top of Oregon moss and on each side of bird's nest, adding more rosebuds to one side of bird's nest than the other.

7. Tie wired ribbon in a bow according to instructions for Making Multi-Loop Bows on page 14.

8. Using hot glue gun and glue sticks, hot-glue bow at top of teardrop. Cascade ribbon tails down each side and hot-glue in place.

Rosebud Topiary

Materials

- Oregon moss
- Rosebuds, dried
- Cinnamon stick: 8"-long
- Styrofoam balls: 2½"-diameter; 3"-diameter
- Creamer & saucer
- Wired ribbon, ⅝"-wide, lavender
- Floral wire
- Craft glue
- Hot glue gun & glue sticks
- Scissors

Instructions

1. Using hot glue gun and glue sticks, hot-glue 3"-diameter styrofoam ball into creamer.

2. Push cinnamon stick into center of styrofoam ball.

3. Push 2½"-diameter styrofoam ball on top of cinnamon stick.

4. Apply craft glue to styrofoam balls and glue Oregon moss around them until both are completely covered.

5. Allow glue to dry thoroughly.

6. Using hot glue gun and glue sticks, hot-glue rosebuds to moss-covered styrofoam ball at top of cinnamon stick until it is completely covered.

7. Tie wired ribbon in a bow according to instructions for Making Multi-Loop Bows on page 14.

8. Using hot glue gun and glue sticks, hot-glue bow to top of cinnamon stick just below styrofoam ball. Cascade ribbon tails down and hot-glue in place.

9. Hot-glue creamer to saucer.

Rosebud Lampshade

Materials

- Lamp shade, natural paper
- Spray stain, oak
- Spanish moss
- Leaves, dried
- Twigs
- Rosebuds, dried
- Rose leaves, dried
- Heather
- Cording, plum
- Acrylic spray, matte
- Adhesive spray
- Hot glue gun & glue sticks

Instructions

1. Make bird's nest according to instructions for Making Bird Nests on page 12.

2. Lightly spray edges of lamp shade with spray stain.

3. Allow spray stain to dry thoroughly.

4. Gather heather and tie cording around center to secure bundle.

5. Tie cording in a bow.

6. Using hot glue gun and glue sticks, hot-glue heather bundle to front of lamp shade at an angle.

7. Hot-glue bird's nest on top of heather bundle.

8. Carefully arrange rosebuds and rose leaves on heather and hot-glue in place.

Rosebud Box Lid

Materials

- Papier-mâché box with lid, hexagon
- Corrugated paper
- Oregon moss
- Rosebuds, dried
- Craft glue

Instructions

1. Apply craft glue to edges of box lid and glue corrugated paper around it. Apply craft glue to top of box lid and glue Oregon moss on it until it is completely covered.

2. Apply craft glue to rosebuds.

3. Carefully arrange rosebuds on top of Oregon moss.

4. Allow glue to dry thoroughly.

Rosebud & Ribbon Wooden Eggs

Materials

- Wooden eggs
- Acrylic paints
- Paintbrush
- Toothbrush
- Foam plate
- Acrylic spray, gloss
- Rosebuds, dried
- Licopodium
- Mesh ribbon
- Toothpick
- Craft glue
- Spanish moss, optional
- Decorative egg carton, optional

Instructions

1. Paint wooden eggs according to instructions for Painting Wooden Eggs on page 13.

2. Tie mesh ribbon around each egg and glue with craft glue to secure.

3. Allow glue to dry thoroughly.

4. Using a toothpick, apply craft glue to back sides of rosebuds and licopodium.

5. Carefully arrange rosebuds and licopodium on front of eggs on top of lace.

6. Allow glue to dry thoroughly.

7. If desired, make one dozen rosebud and lace wooden eggs and display in a decorative egg carton. Spanish moss can be added in the bottom of each "egg cup" to enhance the beauty of the painted and embellished eggs.

Fresh Flowers ...

Roses in a Moss Vase

Photograph on page 53.

Materials

- ❧ Roses, fresh
- ❧ Baby's breath, fresh
- ❧ Spiral picks
- ❧ Oregon moss
- ❧ Decorative charm
- ❧ Mesh ribbon, 2"-wide, gold
- ❧ Poster board, green
- ❧ Vase, round
- ❧ Craft glue
- ❧ Hot glue gun & glue sticks
- ❧ Pencil
- ❧ Measuring tape
- ❧ Stapler & staples
- ❧ Scissors

Instructions

1. Measure vase height and the circumference around vase with measuring tape.

2. Using a pencil, draw a pattern on poster board using the dimensions plus 1" added to length.

3. Cut out pattern with scissors.

4. Arrange roses, baby's breath, and spiral picks inside vase.

5. Apply craft glue to poster board pattern and cover with Oregon moss until it is completely covered.

6. Allow glue to dry thoroughly.

7. Place poster board around vase, overlapping one inch, and staple to secure.

8. Place vase with fresh flower arrangement inside moss-covered "tube."

9. Tie mesh ribbon around moss-covered tube and tie in a bow.

10. Using hot glue gun and glue sticks, hot-glue ribbon and bow to secure. Cascade ribbon tails down and hot-glue in place.

11. Hot-glue decorative charm to front of moss-covered tube just below center of bow.

Curtain Tie Back

Materials

- ❧ Freesia stems, fresh
- ❧ Fern stems, fresh
- ❧ Baby's breath, fresh
- ❧ Sheer ribbon, 3"-wide
- ❧ Floral wire
- ❧ Corsage pins
- ❧ Scissors

Instructions

1. Gather fern stems together and hold tightly around bottom.

2. Gather baby's breath and place on top of fern stems.

3. Place freesia stems on top of baby's breath and cut stems to about 10 inches.

4. Wrap floral wire around bottom of stems to secure bundle.

5. Tie sheer ribbon in a bow according to instructions for Making Multi-Loop Bows on page 14.

6. Wire bow around fresh flower bundle.

7. Pin arrangement to curtain with corsage pins.

8. Note: This tie back will stay fresh for no longer than six to eight hours; it is recommended that this tie back be assembled one hour prior to displaying.

Rose Wreath

Materials

- ❧ Roses, fresh
  pink (12)
  purple (12)
  yellow (12)
- ❧ Tulips, fresh (6)
- ❧ Freesia stems,
  fresh (6)
- ❧ Ivy stems,
  fresh (2)
- ❧ Fern stems,
  fresh (2)
- ❧ Foam floral
  wreath,
  8"-diameter
- ❧ Floral preservative:
  1 tablespoon
- ❧ Leather gloves
- ❧ Pan, shallow
- ❧ Pruning shears

Instructions

1. Fill pan with cold water and add floral preservative.

2. Place foam floral wreath into pan of cold water.

3. Wearing leather gloves, clip rose stems to about 2" in length with pruning shears.

4. Remove foam floral wreath from pan of cold water and place on a flat working surface.

5. Beginning on the inside edge, firmly push roses into wet foam floral wreath.

6. Repeat process until all roses have been placed evenly around wreath.

7. Repeat process for remaining fresh flowers and greenery until all have been used and the wreath is completely covered.

8. Note: This wreath will stay fresh for no longer than one day; it is recommended that this wreath be assembled one hour prior to displaying.

Of all the wonderful things
in the wonderful Universe of God,
nothing seems to me more surprising

than the planting of a seed in the Earth and the blessings thereof.

— *Adapted from Celia Thaxter,
An Island Garden*

Flowers in Fresh Fruit Vases

Materials

- ❦ Flowers, fresh
- ❦ Vases, transparent
- ❦ Limes, fresh
- ❦ Lemons, fresh
- ❦ Oranges, fresh
- ❦ Slicer
- ❦ Kettle

Instructions

1. Slice limes, lemons, and oranges with a slicer into a kettle of cold water.

2. Rinse each slice to remove acid and pulp.

3. Fill vases half full of fresh, cold water.

4. Add some lime, lemon, and orange slices to vases.

5. Arrange fresh flowers inside vases as desired.

6. Add remaining lime, lemon, and orange slices to vases, around arrangements.

7. Fill vases with cold water.

Flowers in Water Pitcher

Materials

❧ Flowers, fresh
❧ Water pitcher

Instructions

1. Choose flowers and water pitcher with the same hue to achieve a mono-chromatic look.

2. Fill water pitcher ²⁄₃ full with cold water.

3. Arrange fresh flowers inside water pitcher as desired.

Plate Garnish

Materials

❧ Flowers, fresh
❧ Ivy stems, fresh
❧ Roses, fresh
❧ Place setting

Instructions

1. Place ivy stems around each dinner plate.

2. Place salad plates and soup bowls on dinner plates and randomly add small fresh flowers on top of ivy stems.

3. De-thorn roses and place one on each dinner plate.

Fresh Flowers Displayed in a Clay Pot & Matching Chair

Materials

- Flowers, fresh
- Vase
- Clay pot
- Wooden chair
- Acrylic paints
- Paintbrush

Instructions

1. Paint clay pot and wooden chair to match with acrylic paints.

2. Allow paints to dry thoroughly.

3. Fill vase ²/₃ full with cold water.

4. Arrange fresh flowers inside vase as desired.

5. Place vase inside clay pot.

6. Hang wooden chair on wall, upside-down.

7. Place clay pot containing fresh flower arrangement into the bottom of the wooden chair.

Beans & Seeds ...

Layered Beans in a Jar

Photograph on page 61.

Materials

- ❧ Jar with cork
- ❧ Kidney beans
- ❧ Garbanzo beans
- ❧ Chile beans
- ❧ Black-eyed peas
- ❧ Black beans
- ❧ Garlic bulb
- ❧ Chile peppers, dried
- ❧ Safflowers, dried
- ❧ German statice
- ❧ Raffia
- ❧ Hot glue gun & glue sticks
- ❧ Hot curling iron

Instructions

1. Layer beans in jar as desired.

2. Place cork on jar.

3. Tie raffia around jar just below cork.

4. Tie raffia in a bow.

5. Using a hot curling iron, curl ends of raffia. <u>Caution: If hot curling iron is left on raffia too long, raffia could ignite.</u>

6. Allow raffia to cool thoroughly and separate raffia ends.

7. Carefully arrange garlic bulb, chile peppers, safflowers, and German statice on top of raffia bow.

8. Using hot glue gun and glue sticks, hot-glue garlic bulb, chile peppers, safflowers, and German statice in place.

Layered Seeds in a Jar

Photograph on page 61.

Materials

- ❧ Jar with cork
- ❧ Poppy seeds
- ❧ Mustard seeds
- ❧ Cardamom seeds
- ❧ Allspice seeds
- ❧ Jute: 3-ply

Instructions

1. Layer seeds in jar as desired.

2. Place cork on jar.

3. Tie jute around cork.

4. Tie jute in a bow and tie knots at each end.

Seed Pomanders

Materials

- ❧ Seeds, as desired
- ❧ Styrofoam balls
- ❧ Raffia or ribbon
- ❧ Craft glue
- ❧ Découpage glue
- ❧ Paintbrush

Instructions

1. Cover styrofoam balls with craft glue.

2. Carefully, but firmly, roll styrofoam balls in seeds.

3. Allow glue to dry thoroughly.

4. Using a paintbrush, apply découpage glue over entire surface of seed pomanders according to manufacturer's directions.

5. Tie raffia or ribbon around styrofoam balls twice, overlapping at center.

Black Bean Box

Materials

- Papier-mâché box with lid, hexagon: 3"-diameter
- Black beans
- Garbanzo beans
- Millet seeds
- Spray stain, cranberry
- Craft glue
- Découpage glue
- Paintbrush

Instructions

1. Spray papier-mâché box and lid with spray stain.

2. Allow spray stain to dry thoroughly.

3. Place lid on box.

4. Apply craft glue to top of box lid and glue black beans around outer edge of box.

5. Fill center of box lid inside black bean border with millet seeds.

6. Glue a cluster of garbanzo beans in center of box lid.

7. Allow glue to dry thoroughly.

8. Using a paint-brush, apply découpage glue over beans and seeds on top of box lid according to manufacturer's directions.

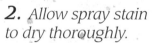

Lima Bean Box

Materials

- Papier-mâché box with lid, hexagon: 3"-diameter
- Lima beans
- Allspice seeds
- Spray stain, green
- Craft glue
- Découpage glue
- Paintbrush

Instructions

1. Spray papier-mâché box and lid with spray stain.

2. Allow spray stain to dry thoroughly.

3. Place lid on box.

4. Apply craft glue to top of box lid and glue lima beans around outer edge of box.

5. Fill center of box lid inside lima bean border with allspice seeds.

6. Allow glue to dry thoroughly.

7. Using a paint-brush, apply découpage glue over beans and seeds on top of box lid according to manufacturer's directions.

Citrus & Sunflowers in a Jar Full of Beans

Materials

- Canning jar: two-quart
- Chile beans: to fill jar
- Sunflowers, dried
- Orange slices, dried
- Garlic bulbs (6)
- Leather fern, dried
- Lemon leaves, dried
- Spanish moss
- Curly willow twigs
- Cinnamon sticks: 12"-long (4)
- Wooden dowels: $1/8$"-diameter, 12"-long (12); $1/4$"-diameter, 12"-long (6)
- Styrofoam ball: 3"-diameter
- Raffia
- Birdhouse on wooden dowel, prepainted
- Coffee pot lid
- Wired ribbon, $2^1/4$"-wide, blue checkered
- Floral wire
- Floral tape, white
- Craft glue
- Hot glue gun & glue sticks
- Scissors

Instructions

1. Fill jar with chile beans.

2. Using hot glue gun and glue sticks, hot-glue styrofoam ball into jar.

3. Apply craft glue to styrofoam ball and glue Spanish moss around it until it is completely covered. Allow some Spanish moss to hang down sides of jar.

4. Push twigs into styrofoam ball.

5. Allow glue to dry thoroughly.

6. Carefully arrange sunflowers, leather fern, and lemon leaves on styrofoam ball. Push sunflowers, leather fern, and lemon leaves into styrofoam ball.

7. Using floral tape, wrap all wooden dowels.

8. Insert $1/4$"-diameter wooden dowels into bottoms of garlic bulbs.

9. Using hot glue gun and glue sticks, hot-glue orange slices to $1/8$"-diameter wooden dowels.

10. Push wooden dowels with garlic bulbs and orange slices on them into styrofoam ball.

11. Braid several strands of raffia and tie knots at each end.

12. Tie raffia braid around neck of jar.

13. Fray ends of raffia.

14. Tie wired ribbon in a bow according to instructions for Making Multi-Loop Bows on page 14.

15. Using hot glue gun and glue sticks, hot-glue bow to right hand side of jar just below neck. Cascade ribbon tails down and hot-glue in place.

16. Position raffia braid on right hand side of jar in center of bow.

17. Gather cinnamon sticks and tie raffia around center to secure bundle.

18. Using hot glue gun and glue sticks, hot-glue cinnamon sticks into side of arrangement.

19. Hot-glue coffee pot lid on top of cinnamon sticks.

20. Push birdhouse on wooden dowel into center of arrangement.

21. Fill hole in front of birdhouse with Spanish moss.

Pinecone & Sunflower Seed Star Ornament

Materials

- Pinecones (5)
- Sunflower seeds (5)
- Pecan
- Mustard seeds
- Jute, waxed
- Cardboard
- Craft glue
- Hot glue gun & glue sticks
- Scissors

Instructions

1. Cut a 1"-diameter cardboard circle with scissors.

2. Using hot glue gun and glue sticks, hot-glue pinecones to outside of cardboard circle to form a star.

3. Hot-glue pecan to cardboard circle inside center of pinecone star.

4. Hot-glue sunflower seeds on top of pinecones to form a star.

5. Apply craft glue to pecan and cover with mustard seeds.

6. Allow glue to dry thoroughly.

7. Attach jute for hanging.

Cinnamon Stick & Fennel Seed Star Ornament

Materials

- Papier-mâché star
- Cinnamon sticks
- Pinecones: tiny
- Fennel seeds
- Jute, waxed
- Craft glue

Instructions

1. Apply craft glue to top of papier-mâché star.

2. Carefully arrange cinnamon sticks around outside edges of star, breaking cinnamon sticks into various lengths as necessary.

3. Allow glue to dry thoroughly.

4. Apply craft glue to top of papier-mâché star.

5. Carefully arrange pinecones around inside edge of cinnamon sticks. Cover remaining area with fennel seeds.

6. Allow glue to dry thoroughly.

7. Attach jute for hanging.

Lima Bean Birdhouse

Materials

- Birdhouse with one or more openings
- Leaves, dried
- Berries, dried
- Twigs
- Lima beans
- Wooden hearts
- Craft glue

Instructions

1. Crumble leaves.

2. Apply craft glue around and inside opening(s) on birdhouse.

3. Carefully sprinkle crumbled leaves around and inside opening(s) on birdhouse.

4. Glue berries, twigs, and lima beans in or near opening(s) on birdhouse.

5. Glue wooden hearts on birdhouse as desired.

6. Allow glue to dry thoroughly.

Sunflower Seed & Barbed Wire Hanger

Materials

- ❧ Sunflower seed head, dried
- ❧ Nuts, assorted
- ❧ Pinecones
- ❧ Cinnamon sticks
- ❧ Log slab
- ❧ Barbed wire
- ❧ Hammer
- ❧ Nails
- ❧ Craft glue
- ❧ Hot glue gun & glue sticks

Instructions

1. Bend barbed wire and nail to sides of log slab to make a handle for hanging.

2. Apply craft glue to back side of sunflower seed head and glue to top of log slab, centered.

3. Allow glue to dry thoroughly.

4. Carefully arrange nuts, pinecones, and cinnamon sticks around right side of sunflower seed head.

5. Using hot glue gun and glue sticks, hot-glue nuts, pinecones, and cinnamon sticks in place.

Fruits & Nuts ...

Dried Fruit in a Jar

Photograph on page 69.

Materials

- ❦ Jar with cork
- ❦ Currants, dried
- ❦ Pineapple, dried
- ❦ Dates, dried
- ❦ Golden raisins
- ❦ Cranberries, dried
- ❦ Licopodium
- ❦ Cedar rose
- ❦ Pinecones
- ❦ Raffia
- ❦ Cording, gold
- ❦ Hot glue gun & glue sticks

Instructions

1. Layer dried fruit in jar as desired.

2. Place cork on jar.

3. Tie raffia around jar just below cork.

4. Tie raffia in a bow.

5. Carefully arrange and hot-glue licopodium, cedar rose, and pinecones on top of raffia bow.

6. Tie cording in a bow and hot-glue into center of arrangement on top of raffia bow.

Woodland Potpourri

Not Photographed

Materials

- ❦ Acorns & acorn hulls
- ❦ Bay leaves, dried
- ❦ Nuts, assorted
- ❦ Pinecones
- ❦ Pomegranates, dried
- ❦ Poppy pods, dried
- ❦ River birch cones
- ❦ Rose hips, dried
- ❦ Fragrance oil: potpourri, 1 ounce
- ❦ Container

Instructions

1. Mix all ingredients together in container with hands.

2. As fragrance dissipates, add more fragrance oil to dried mixture.

3. If desired, display a seed pomander on top of potpourri or tie a few cinnamon sticks together with raffia and place on top of potpourri. See Seed Pomanders on page 62.

Citrus & Spice Potpourri

Materials

- ❦ Cinnamon sticks, broken: 2 cups
- ❦ Grapefruit slices, dried: 1 cup
- ❦ Calendula, dried: 1 cup
- ❦ Orange rind
- ❦ Orange slices, dried: 1 cup
- ❦ Orris root, dried: 1 tablespoon
- ❦ River birch cones: 1 cup
- ❦ Rose hips, dried: 1 cup
- ❦ Spiced ornaments, heart-shaped & star-shaped
- ❦ Star anise, dried: 1 cup
- ❦ Fragrance oil: tangerine, 1 ounce
- ❦ Cookie cutters, heart-shaped & star-shaped
- ❦ Container

Instructions

1. Make heart- and star-shaped spiced ornaments according to instructions for Making Spiced Ornaments on page 15.

2. Using a star-shaped cookie cutter, cut stars from orange rind.

3. Allow orange rind stars to dry thoroughly.

4. Mix all ingredients together in container with hands.

5. As fragrance dissipates, add more fragrance oil to dried mixture.

Citrus & Spice Potpourri in a Jar

Materials

- Jar with cork
- Pressed flowers
- Pressed greenery
- Cinnamon stick
- Orange slice, dried
- Citrus & spice potpourri
- Raffia
- Ground cinnamon: 1 cup
- Ground cloves: 1 tablespoon
- Ground nutmeg: 1 tablespoon
- Applesauce: 3/4 cup
- All-purpose glue: 2 tablespoons
- Water: 3/4 to 1 cup
- Jute, waxed
- Tweezers
- Toothpick
- Craft glue
- Découpage glue
- Paintbrush
- Cookie cutter, heart-shaped
- Mixing bowl
- Wooden spoon
- Cookie sheet

Instructions

1. Fill jar with citrus and spice potpourri. See Citrus and Spice Potpourri on page 70.

2. Make heart-shaped spiced ornaments according to instructions for Making Spiced Ornaments on page 15.

3. String heart-shaped spiced ornaments onto jute so they hang nicely.

4. Place cork on jar. Photograph shows cork removed from jar to show details.

5. Tie raffia around jar just below cork.

6. Place a cinnamon stick in the center and tie raffia in a bow.

7. Hang heart-shaped spiced ornaments from raffia bow.

8. Apply craft glue to back side of orange slice.

9. Carefully arrange orange slice on top of raffia bow.

10. Allow glue to dry thoroughly.

11. Using tweezers, pick up pressed flowers and greenery.

12. Using a toothpick, apply craft glue to back sides of pressed flowers and greenery.

13. Carefully arrange pressed flowers and greenery on top of cork.

14. Allow glue to dry thoroughly.

15. Using a paintbrush, apply découpage glue over pressed flowers and greenery on top of cork according to manufacturer's directions.

Citrus in a Water Pitcher

Materials

- ❧ Water pitcher
- ❧ Orange slices, dried
- ❧ Rosebuds, dried
- ❧ Globe amaranth, dried
- ❧ Nigella, dried
- ❧ Yarrow, dried
- ❧ Lantern pods, dried
- ❧ German statice
- ❧ Statice sinuata
- ❧ Lemon leaves, dried
- ❧ Myrtle leaves, dried
- ❧ Heather
- ❧ Curly willow twigs
- ❧ Deer moss
- ❧ Styrofoam ball: to fit water pitcher opening
- ❧ Wired ribbons: 1"-wide, lavender iridescent; 3/4"-wide, green checkered
- ❧ Floral wire
- ❧ Craft glue
- ❧ Hot glue gun & glue sticks
- ❧ Scissors

Instructions

1. Using hot glue gun and glue sticks, hot-glue styrofoam ball into water pitcher.

2. Apply craft glue to styrofoam ball and glue deer moss around it until it is completely covered. Allow some deer moss to hang down sides of water pitcher.

3. Allow glue to dry thoroughly.

4. Push heather and twigs into styrofoam ball.

5. Using hot glue gun and glue sticks, carefully arrange and hot-glue orange slices, rosebuds, globe amaranth, nigella, yarrow, lantern pods, German statice, statice sinuata, lemon leaves, and myrtle leaves on top of moss-covered styrofoam ball.

6. Tie wired ribbons in bows according to instructions for Making Multi-Loop Bows on page 14.

7. Using hot glue gun and glue sticks, hot-glue lavender iridescent bow to side of water pitcher next to handle. Cascade ribbon tails down.

8. Hot-glue green checkered bow on top of lavender iridescent bow. Cascade ribbon tails down.

Orange & Nut Ornaments

Materials

- ❧ Orange rind
- ❧ Pecans
- ❧ Whole nutmeg
- ❧ Jute, waxed
- ❧ Cookie cutter, star-shaped
- ❧ Needle with large eye
- ❧ Drill with 1/16" drill bit
- ❧ Scissors

Instructions

1. Drill a hole through center of each nut with drill and 1/16" drill bit.

2. Using a star-shaped cookie cutter, cut stars from orange rind and make a hole in the center of each star.

3. Allow orange rind stars to dry thoroughly.

4. For each ornament, cut jute with scissors to twice the desired length. Double strand the jute and tie a knot at end.

5. Thread double strand of jute onto needle.

6. String pecans, orange rind stars, and whole nutmeg onto jute. Push down so pecans rest on knots. Use loops at top for hanging.

Apples & Juniper Berries in a Crate

Materials

- ❧ Wooden crate, oblong
- ❧ Nigella, dried
- ❧ Apple slices, dried
- ❧ Juniper berries, dried
- ❧ Lantern pods, dried
- ❧ Cinnamon sticks
- ❧ Oregon moss
- ❧ Hot glue gun & glue sticks

Instructions

1. Break cinnamon sticks into uniform lengths.

2. Using hot glue gun and glue sticks, hot-glue Oregon moss into bottom of wooden crate.

3. Carefully arrange and hot-glue nigella around outside edges of wooden crate on top of Oregon moss.

4. Hot-glue apple slices in a border inside nigella, followed by cinnamon sticks and juniper berries. Hot-glue lantern pods into center of juniper berry border.

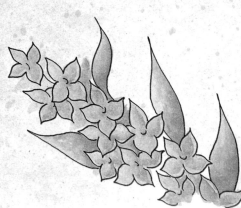

Apples & Rosebuds in a Basket

Materials

- Twig basket
- Apple slices, dried
- Rosebuds, dried
- Rose leaves, dried
- Twigs
- Baby's breath, dried
- Oregon moss
- Floral foam for drieds, to fit inside basket
- Floral pins
- Wired ribbon, 1"-wide, red-yellow ombré
- Floral wire
- Hot glue gun & glue sticks
- Scissors

Instructions

1. Place floral foam inside basket, making certain it fits tightly all the way around the edges.

2. Using floral pins, cover floral foam with Oregon moss until it is completely covered.

3. Using hot glue gun and glue sticks, hot-glue rosebuds, rose leaves, and baby's breath into basket.

4. Hot-glue apple slices around edges of basket and into center of arrangement.

5. Push twigs into floral foam.

6. Tie wired ribbon in a bow according to instructions for Making Multi-Loop Bows on page 14.

7. Using hot glue gun and glue sticks, hot-glue bow to top of basket. Cascade ribbon tails down each side and hot-glue in place.

Apples & Cinnamon Sticks

Materials

- ❦ Apple slices, dried
- ❦ Ammobium, dried
- ❦ Statice sinuata
- ❦ Cinnamon sticks
- ❦ Ground cinnamon: 1 cup
- ❦ Ground cloves: 1 tablespoon
- ❦ Ground nutmeg: 1 tablespoon
- ❦ Applesauce: ³/₄ cup
- ❦ All-purpose glue: 2 tablespoons
- ❦ Water: ³/₄ to 1 cup
- ❦ Wired ribbon, ³/₄"-wide, blue-green ombré
- ❦ Floral wire
- ❦ Jute, waxed
- ❦ Toothpick
- ❦ Cookie cutter, heart-shaped
- ❦ Mixing bowl
- ❦ Wooden spoon
- ❦ Cookie sheet
- ❦ Hot glue gun & glue sticks
- ❦ Scissors

Instructions

1. Make heart-shaped spiced ornaments according to instructions for Making Spiced Ornaments on page 15.

2. Gather cinnamon sticks and tie jute around center to secure bundle.

3. Tie wired ribbon in a bow according to instructions for Making Multi-Loop Bows on page 14.

4. Using hot glue gun and glue sticks, hot-glue bow centered on top of cinnamon sticks.

5. Carefully arrange and hot-glue statice sinuata and ammo-bium on top of cinnamon sticks on each side of bow. Make certain the arrangement is even on both sides.

6. Hot-glue apple slices into center of arrangement just above bow.

7. String heart-shaped spiced ornaments onto jute so they hang nicely.

8. Using hot glue gun and glue sticks, hot-glue spiced ornaments into center of arrangement on top of wired-ribbon bow.

Apples & Garlic in a Salt Shaker

Materials

- Salt shaker with lid
- Apple slices, dried
- Garlic bulb
- Ammobium, dried
- Poppy pods, dried
- Myrtle leaves, dried
- Oregon moss
- Cinnamon sticks
- Ground cinnamon: 1 cup
- Ground cloves: 1 tablespoon
- Ground nutmeg: 1 tablespoon
- Applesauce: ³/₄ cup
- All-purpose glue: 2 tablespoons
- Water: ³/₄ to 1 cup
- Styrofoam ball: to fit salt shaker opening
- Wired ribbon, ³/₄"-wide, dark green
- Floral wire
- Copper wire: 19-gauge
- Birdhouse on wooden dowel
- Tree bark
- Jute, waxed
- Toothpick
- Cookie cutter, heart-shaped
- Mixing bowl
- Wooden spoon
- Cookie sheet
- Craft glue
- Hot glue gun & glue sticks
- Scissors

Instructions

1. Make heart-shaped spiced ornaments according to instructions for Making Spiced Ornaments on page 15.

2. Using hot glue gun and glue sticks, hot-glue styrofoam ball into salt shaker.

3. Push wooden dowel with birdhouse attached into center of styrofoam ball.

4. Apply craft glue to styrofoam ball and glue Oregon moss around it until it is completely covered.

5. Allow glue to dry thoroughly.

6. Using hot glue gun and glue sticks, carefully arrange and hot-glue apple slices, garlic bulb, ammobium, poppy pods, myrtle leaves, and cinnamon sticks on top of moss-covered styrofoam ball.

7. Hot-glue tree bark to both sides of birdhouse roof.

8. Form a copper wire loop through one of the holes in top of salt shaker lid.

9. Twist copper wire at top to secure, leaving a two-inch long tail.

10. Push copper wire tail into styrofoam ball, hanging salt shaker lid on side of salt shaker.

11. Tie wired ribbon in a bow according to instructions for Making Multi-Loop Bows on page 14.

12. Using hot glue gun and glue sticks, hot-glue bow into arrangement just above salt shaker lid.

13. String heart-shaped spiced ornaments onto jute so they hang nicely.

14. Using hot glue gun and glue sticks, hot-glue spiced ornaments into arrangement on top of wired-ribbon bow.

Pecan & Nutmeg Wind Chime

Materials

- Pecans
- Whole nutmeg
- Cinnamon sticks
- Jute: 3-ply
- Clay pots: ½"-diameter (3)
- Needle with large eye
- Drill with ¼" drill bit
- Scissors

Instructions

1. Drill a hole through center of each nut and cinnamon stick with drill and ¼" drill bit.

2. Cut jute with scissors.

3. Tie a knot about 3" down from top to make a loop for hanging.

4. Thread jute onto needle.

5. String one pecan onto jute and tie a knot under it. String three cinnamon sticks onto jute and tie a knot under them. String one whole nutmeg onto jute and tie a knot under it.

6. String one clay pot upside-down onto jute and tie a knot under it. Repeat process for remaining two clay pots.

7. Tie a knot in jute just below rim of third clay pot. String one whole nutmeg onto jute and tie a knot under it. String one pecan onto jute and tie a knot under it.

8. Fray ends of jute.

Pinecone & Chestnut Topiary

Materials

- ❧ Oregon moss
- ❧ Chestnuts
- ❧ Nuts, assorted
- ❧ Pinecones
- ❧ Cinnamon sticks: 8"-long
- ❧ Jute: 2-ply
- ❧ Clay pot: 4"-diameter
- ❧ Styrofoam cone: 3"-diameter
- ❧ Styrofoam ball: 4"-diameter
- ❧ Craft glue
- ❧ Hot glue gun & glue sticks

Instructions

1. Using hot glue gun and glue sticks, hot-glue styrofoam ball into clay pot.

2. Hot-glue four cinnamon sticks together and push into center of styrofoam ball.

3. Push styrofoam cone, pointed end up, on top of cinnamon sticks.

4. Apply craft glue to styrofoam ball and styrofoam cone and glue Oregon moss around them until they are completely covered.

5. Allow glue to dry thoroughly.

6. Break cinnamon sticks into two-inch lengths.

7. Using hot glue gun and glue sticks, carefully arrange and hot-glue chestnuts, nuts, pinecones, and 2"-long cinnamon sticks to moss-covered styrofoam cone at top of cinnamon sticks until it is completely covered.

8. Tie jute around cinnamon sticks.

9. Tie jute in a bow and tie knots at each end.

Cookie Cutter Centerpieces

Materials

- Cranberries, dried
- Pinecones
- Oregon moss
- Acrylic paints:
  Copper
  Green
- Sponge
- Wooden dowels:
  ¹/₄"-diameter,
  4"-long (3)
- Clay pots with
  saucers:
  5"-diameter (3)
- Cookie cutters,
  metal,
  gingerbread
  man-, tree-,
  and star-shaped
- Plaster of paris
- Hammer
- Nails
- Hot glue gun &
  glue sticks

Instructions

1. Mix plaster of paris according to manufacturer's directions.

2. Pour plaster of paris into clay pots. Fill to just below rim.

3. Insert wooden dowels into center of each clay pot.

4. Allow plaster of paris to harden.

5. Using a sponge, sponge-paint

wooden dowels and clay pots and saucers with acrylic paints.

6. Allow paints to dry thoroughly.

7. Using hot glue gun and glue sticks, hot-glue clay pots to saucers.

8. Hot-glue Oregon moss inside clay pots until plaster of

paris is completely covered and the moss is in a mound at the top.

9. Carefully arrange and hot-glue cranberries and pinecones on top of Oregon moss, as desired.

10. If desired, metal cookie cutters can be "aged" by soak-

ing them in water overnight.

11. Center cookie cutters on top of wooden dowels, and nail in place.

12. Using hot glue gun and glue sticks, hot-glue star-shaped cookie cutter to top of tree-shaped cookie cutter.

Pomegranate & Pepper Berries Wreath

Materials

- ❦ Pomegranates, dried
- ❦ Rosebuds, dried
- ❦ Sunflowers, dried
- ❦ Garlic bulbs
- ❦ Pepper berries, dried
- ❦ Cockscomb, dried
- ❦ Lemon leaves, dried
- ❦ Deer moss
- ❦ Twigs
- ❦ Branches, green
- ❦ Copper wire: 19-gauge
- ❦ Wired ribbon, 1¹/₂"-wide, purple iridescent
- ❦ Floral wire
- ❦ Hot glue gun & glue sticks
- ❦ Scissors

Instructions

1. Bend green branches into desired shape and secure them with copper wire.

2. Using hot glue gun and glue sticks, carefully arrange and hot-glue lemon leaves around outside edges of wreath.

3. Hot-glue deer moss to wreath inside lemon leaves.

4. Carefully arrange and hot-glue pomegranates, rosebuds, sunflowers, garlic bulbs, pepper berries, and cockscomb to wreath on top of deer moss.

5. Randomly hot-glue twigs into arrangement.

6. Tie wired ribbon in a bow according to instructions for Making Multi-Loop Bows on page 14.

7. Using hot glue gun and glue sticks, hot-glue bow to wreath. Cascade ribbon tails down.

Grapefruit & Apple Garland

Materials

- Grapefruit slices, dried
- Apple slices, dried
- Cinnamon sticks
- Pinecones
- Acrylic paint: Yellow-gold
- Paintbrush
- Papier-mâché stars
- Jute, waxed
- Jute: 2-ply
- Spray stain, oak
- Needle with large eye
- Drill with ⅛" drill bit

Instructions

1. Using a paintbrush, paint papier-mâché stars with yellow-gold acrylic paint.

2. Allow paint to dry thoroughly.

3. Spray papier-mâché stars with spray stain.

4. Allow spray stain to dry thoroughly.

5. Drill a hole through center of each cinnamon stick and star with drill and ⅛" drill bit.

6. Tie waxed jute tightly around each pinecone. Tie a knot at ends to make a loop for hanging.

7. Thread 2-ply jute onto needle and tie a knot six inches from one end.

8. String items onto 2-ply jute in the following order: two cinnamon sticks, two pinecones (through waxed jute loops), one grapefruit slice, three apple slices, one more grapefruit slice, two more pinecones, two more cinnamon sticks, and one papier-mâché star. Push down so the first cinnamon stick rests on knot.

9. Repeat process until garland is the desired length and tie a knot six inches from end. If more 2-ply jute is needed to complete garland, tie another piece of 2-ply jute to existing piece and tie a knot to secure. Make certain the needle is on the new piece of 2-ply jute.

10. Double the 2-ply jute at each end and tie a knot to make loops for hanging.

11. Randomly tie two knots at each end of 2-ply jute.

Grapefruit & Bay Leaf Garland

Photograph on page 82.

Materials

- Grapefruit slices, dried
- Bay leaves, dried
- Cinnamon sticks
- Pinecones
- Deer moss
- Clay pots: 3"-diameter
- Jute, waxed
- Raffia, optional
- Needle with large eye
- Hot glue gun & glue sticks
- Drill with $^1/_8$" drill bit

Instructions

1. Drill a hole through center of each cinnamon stick and sides of clay pots with drill and $^1/_8$" drill bit.

2. Tie waxed jute tightly around each pinecone. Tie a knot at ends to make a loop for hanging.

3. Thread jute onto needle and tie a large knot six inches from one end.

4. String items onto jute in the following order: one cinnamon stick, several bay leaves, one pinecone (through waxed jute loops), several more bay leaves, one more pinecone, several more bay leaves, three grapefruit slices, several more bay leaves, one clay pot, several more bay leaves, three more grapefruit slices, several more bay leaves, and one more pinecone. Push down so the cinnamon stick rests on knot.

5. Reverse the order without adding a second pinecone to the center.

6. Repeat process until garland is the desired length and tie a knot six inches from end. If more jute is needed to complete garland, tie another piece of jute to existing piece and tie a knot to secure. Make certain the needle is on the new piece of jute.

7. Double the jute at each end and tie a knot to make loops for hanging.

8. Using hot glue gun and glue sticks, hot-glue deer moss inside each clay pot.

9. If desired, randomly tie raffia bows around waxed jute.

Chestnut Garland

Materials

- Chestnuts
- Pinecones
- Jute, waxed
- Jute: 3-ply
- Needle with large eye
- Drill with $^1/_8$" drill bit

Instructions

1. Drill a hole through center of each chestnut with drill and $^1/_8$" drill bit.

2. Tie waxed jute tightly around each pinecone. Tie a knot at ends to make a loop for hanging.

3. Thread waxed jute onto needle and tie a large knot six inches from one end.

4. String items onto waxed jute in the following order: five chestnuts and three pinecones (through waxed jute loops). Push down so the first chestnut rests on knot.

5. Repeat process until garland is the desired length and tie a knot six inches from end. If more waxed jute is needed to complete garland, tie another piece of waxed jute to existing piece and tie a knot to secure. Make certain the needle is on the new piece of waxed jute.

6. Double the waxed jute at each end and tie a knot to make loops for hanging.

7. Tie 3-ply jute in two bows and tie around waxed jute at each end of garland.

Dried Fruit & Pinecone Topiary

Materials

- ❦ Oregon moss
- ❦ Apple slices, dried
- ❦ Orange slices, dried
- ❦ Pomegranates, dried
- ❦ Yarrow, dried
- ❦ Myrtle leaves, dried
- ❦ Pinecones
- ❦ Cinnamon sticks: 8"-long
- ❦ Watering can, tin
- ❦ Styrofoam balls: 2½"-diameter; 3"-diameter
- ❦ Wired ribbon, ¾"-wide, copper iridescent
- ❦ Floral wire
- ❦ Craft glue
- ❦ Hot glue gun & glue sticks
- ❦ Scissors

Instructions

1. Using hot glue gun and glue sticks, hot-glue 3"-diameter styrofoam ball into watering can.

2. Hot-glue three cinnamon sticks together and push into center of styrofoam ball.

3. Push 2½"-diameter styrofoam ball on top of cinnamon sticks.

4. Apply craft glue to styrofoam balls and glue Oregon moss around them until both are completely covered.

5. Allow glue to dry thoroughly.

6. Using hot glue gun and glue sticks, carefully arrange and hot-glue apple slices, orange slices, pomegranates, yarrow, myrtle leaves, and pinecones to moss-covered styrofoam ball at top of cinnamon sticks until it is completely covered.

7. Tie wired ribbon in a bow according to instructions for Making Multi-Loop Bows on page 14.

8. Using hot glue gun and glue sticks, hot-glue bow to top of moss-covered styrofoam ball in watering can. Cascade ribbon tails down and hot-glue in place.

9. Carefully arrange and hot-glue pinecones, cinnamon sticks, one apple slice, and one orange slice to top of moss-covered styrofoam ball just behind bow.

Herbs ...

Baby Dill & Chile Pepper Vinegar

Photograph on page 85.

Materials

- Bottle with wire closure
- Carrots with carrot tops: thin (3)
- Baby dill sprig
- Chile peppers (2)
- Garlic cloves (2)
- Vinegar, white: see steps 1 & 2
- Vinegar, apple cider: see steps 1 & 2
- Non-iodized salt: 1 teaspoon
- Sugar, optional: 1 teaspoon
- Measuring cup: 1 cup
- Saucepan
- Funnel
- Scissors

Instructions

1. To determine how much vinegar the bottle will hold, measure by filling bottle up with water using a measuring cup.

2. The amount of vinegar to be used is based on a 3:1 ratio. Three parts of white vinegar to one part of apple cider vinegar.

3. Wash and sterilize bottle.

4. Place white vinegar, apple cider vinegar, salt, and sugar in a saucepan and bring to a boil.

5. Wash carrots, baby dill sprig, and chile peppers.

6. Trim carrot tops with scissors leaving two to three inches.

7. Remove skins around garlic cloves.

8. Drop chile peppers and garlic cloves into sterilized bottle.

9. Place carrots and baby dill sprig in bottle. The carrots must fit nicely in bottle.

10. Using a funnel, carefully pour hot vinegar into bottle. The chile peppers, garlic cloves, carrots, and baby dill sprig will float to top of bottle, but will settle on bottom in about two weeks. <u>Note: Make certain carrots are submerged in vinegar.</u>

11. Wipe mouth of bottle and seal with wire closure.

12. It is recommended that this vinegar be used within two months.

Wheat & Straw Flowers in a Jar

Photograph on page 85.

Materials

- Bottle with cork
- Wheat stem, dried
- Globe amaranth, dried
- Mineral or baby oil
- Funnel
- Beeswax or paraffin wax
- Saucepan
- Tin can
- Pliers
- Salad tongs
- Waxed paper

Instructions

1. Place wheat stem and globe amaranth in bottle.

2. Using a funnel, carefully pour mineral or baby oil into bottle.

3. Wipe mouth of bottle and seal with cork.

4. Melt wax according to instructions for Melting Wax on page 10.

5. Using salad tongs, turn bottle upside-down and dip cork and top of bottle into hot wax several times until desired look is achieved.

Rosemary, Sage & Thyme Vinegar

Photograph on page 85.

Materials

- Bottle with cork
- Rosemary stem
- Sage sprig
- Thyme sprig
- Vinegar, white
- Saucepan
- Funnel

Instructions

1. Wash and sterilize bottle.

2. Place vinegar in a saucepan and bring to a boil.

3. Wash rosemary stem, sage sprig, and thyme sprig. Pat dry.

4. Place rosemary stem, sage sprig, and thyme sprig in bottle.

5. Using a funnel, carefully pour hot vinegar into bottle. The herbs will float to top of bottle, but will settle on bottom in about two weeks.

6. Wipe mouth of bottle and seal with cork.

7. It is recommended that this vinegar be used within two months.

Garlic & Basil Vinegar

Materials

- ❦ Bottle with cork
- ❦ Garlic cloves (2)
- ❦ Basil, dried: small bunch
- ❦ Rice vinegar, seasoned
- ❦ Saucepan
- ❦ Funnel

Instructions

1. Wash and sterilize bottle.

2. Place rice vinegar in a saucepan and bring to a boil.

3. Remove skins around garlic cloves.

4. Drop garlic cloves into sterilized bottle.

5. Place basil in bottle.

6. Using a funnel, carefully pour hot vinegar into bottle. The garlic cloves and basil will float to top of bottle, but will settle on bottom in about two weeks.

7. Wipe mouth of bottle and seal with cork.

8. It is recommended that this vinegar be used within two months.

Garlic & Basil Vinegar Salad

Not Photographed

Ingredients

- Romaine lettuce, 4 cups torn
- Red onion, $^1/_2$ cup sliced
- Jumbo olives, 1 can sliced
- Basil, dried: 2 tablespoons
- Parsley leaves, 1 teaspoon
- Feta cheese, $^1/_2$ cup crumbled
- Olive oil
- Garlic & basil vinegar
- Salt & pepper

Instructions

1. Wash romaine lettuce. Pat dry.

2. Place romaine lettuce, red onion, olives, basil leaves, parsley leaves, and feta cheese in a salad bowl.

3. Toss lightly and add olive oil and garlic and basil vinegar. See Garlic and Basil Vinegar on page 87.

4. Salt and pepper to taste.

Foxtail Millet & Chile Pepper Spray

Materials

- Foxtail millet, dried
- Chile peppers, dried
- Garlic bulb
- Straw flowers
- Safflowers, dried
- Galoxa leaves, dried
- Raffia
- Hot glue gun & glue sticks

Instructions

1. Gather foxtail millet and tie raffia around center to secure bundle.

2. Tie raffia in a bow.

3. Using hot glue gun and glue sticks, hot-glue galoxa leaves to foxtail millet bundle just above raffia bow.

4. Carefully arrange and hot-glue chile peppers, garlic bulb, straw flowers, and safflowers on top of galoxa leaves and on top of raffia bow.

Chile Pepper Star

Materials

- Chile peppers, dried
- Garlic bulbs
- Bay leaves, dried
- Branches, straight (5)
- Jute, waxed
- Floral wire

Instructions

1. Arrange branches into a star shape and secure at points with floral wire.

2. Carefully thread chile peppers onto floral wire to create a garland long enough to fit across front of star.

3. Wire chile pepper garland to front of star so it hangs nicely.

4. Carefully thread garlic bulbs and bay leaves onto floral wire to create a garland long enough to fit across front of star.

5. Wire garlic bulb and bay leaf garland to front of star just above chile pepper garland so it hangs nicely.

6. Cover floral wire at star points with jute.

Chile Pepper Garland

Materials

- Chile peppers, dried
- Oregon moss
- Raffia
- Wooden rake
- Clay pot
- Floral foam for drieds, to fit inside clay pot
- Floral pins
- Floral wire
- Spray stain, green
- Hot glue gun & glue sticks

Instructions

1. Spray wooden rake with spray stain.

2. Allow spray stain to dry thoroughly.

3. Carefully thread chile peppers onto floral wire to create a garland.

4. Wire chile pepper garland to front of wooden rake so it hangs nicely.

5. Tie raffia in a bow and hot-glue to wooden rake as desired.

6. Place floral foam inside clay pot, making certain it fits tightly all the way around the edges.

7. Using floral pins, cover floral foam with Oregon moss until it is completely covered.

8. Push wooden rake into floral foam inside clay pot.

Bay Leaf & Seed Pomander Garland

Materials

- ❧ Bay leaves, dried
- ❧ Apple slices, dried
- ❧ Seeds, as desired
- ❧ Styrofoam balls
- ❧ Jute, waxed
- ❧ Raffia or ribbon
- ❧ Craft glue
- ❧ Découpage glue
- ❧ Paintbrush
- ❧ Needle with large eye

Instructions

1. Make seed pomanders. See Seed Pomanders on page 62.

2. Thread jute onto needle and tie a knot six inches from one end.

3. String items onto jute in the following order: several bay leaves, one apple slice, several more bay leaves, and one seed pomander. Push first bunch of bay leaves down so it rests on knot.

4. Repeat process until garland is the desired length and tie a knot six inches from end. If more jute is needed to complete garland, tie another piece of jute to existing piece and tie a knot to secure. Make certain the needle is on the new piece of jute.

5. Double the jute at each end and tie a knot to make loops for hanging.

Garlic Bulbs in a Crate

Materials

- Wooden crate, oblong
- Pomegranate, dried
- Ammobium, dried
- Lantern pods, dried
- Pinecones
- Garlic bulbs
- Nigella, dried
- Safflowers, dried
- Cinnamon sticks
- Oregon moss
- Raffia
- Hot glue gun & glue sticks

Instructions

1. Break cinnamon sticks into uniform lengths.

2. Divide wooden crate into eight equal sections with raffia.

3. Using hot glue gun and glue sticks, hot-glue Oregon moss into bottom of wooden crate in all eight sections.

4. Hot-glue the pomegranate into the first section on top of Oregon moss.

5. Hot-glue ammobium into the second section on top of Oregon moss until it is completely full.

6. Hot-glue lantern pods into the third section on top of Oregon moss until it is completely full.

7. Hot-glue pinecones into the fourth section on top of Oregon moss until it is completely full.

8. Hot-glue garlic bulbs into the fifth section on top of Oregon moss.

9. Hot-glue nigella into the sixth section on top of Oregon moss until it is completely full.

10. Hot-glue safflowers into the seventh section on top of Oregon moss until it is completely full.

11. Hot-glue cinnamon sticks into the eighth section on top of Oregon moss until it is completely full.

Garlic Bulb Topiary

Materials

- ❦ Garlic bulbs
- ❦ Chile peppers, dried
- ❦ Bay leaves, dried
- ❦ Deer moss
- ❦ Raffia
- ❦ Wooden dowels: $^1/_8$"-diameter
- ❦ Clay pot: 4"-diameter
- ❦ Styrofoam cone: 3"-diameter
- ❦ Styrofoam ball: 4"-diameter
- ❦ Floral tape, white
- ❦ Craft glue
- ❦ Hot glue gun & glue sticks

Instructions

1. Using hot glue gun and glue sticks, hot-glue styrofoam ball into clay pot.

2. Roll styrofoam cone on top of a hard surface to flatten the point.

3. Using hot glue gun and glue sticks, hot-glue styrofoam cone to styrofoam ball, with the cone point up.

4. Apply craft glue to styrofoam ball and styrofoam cone and glue deer moss

around them until they are completely covered.

5. Allow glue to dry thoroughly.

6. Using floral tape, wrap all wooden dowels.

7. Insert wooden dowels into tops of garlic bulbs.

8. Push wooden dowels with garlic bulbs on them into styrofoam ball. <u>Note: Begin at the top and work down in a circular pattern.</u>

9. Using hot glue gun and glue sticks, carefully arrange and hot-glue chile peppers and bay

leaves to moss-covered styrofoam cone in between garlic bulbs.

10. Tie raffia in a bow and hot-glue to side of clay pot just below arrangement.

Garlic Bulb & German Statice Garland

Materials

- ❦ Garlic bulbs
- ❦ German statice
- ❦ Raffia
- ❦ Hot glue gun & glue sticks
- ❦ Needle with large eye
- ❦ Scissors

Instructions

1. Cut raffia with scissors to twice the desired length. Double strand the raffia and tie a knot at end.

2. Thread double strand of raffia onto needle.

3. String garlic bulbs onto raffia. Push down so the first garlic bulb rests on knot.

4. Leaving a loop at the top for hanging, braid several new strands of raffia. Intertwine around garlic bulbs and tie a knot at the end.

5. Fray ends of raffia.

6. Using hot glue gun and glue sticks, hot-glue German statice to raffia braid in between garlic bulbs.

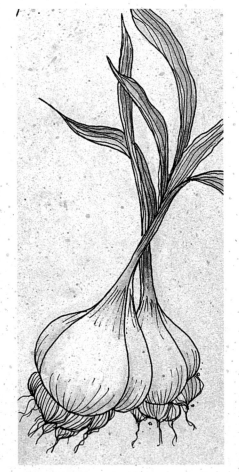

Harvest ...

Corn Husk Doll

Photograph on page 95.

Materials

- ❧ Corn husks, dried
- ❧ Styrofoam ball: $^7/_8$"-diameter
- ❧ Floral wire, heavy
- ❧ Wool doll hair
- ❧ Fabric, plaid
- ❧ Straw hat
- ❧ Thread
- ❧ Accessories, as desired
- ❧ Hot glue gun & glue sticks
- ❧ Towel
- ❧ Scissors

Instructions

Doll's Head

1. Soak corn husks in warm water until pliable — about 10 minutes.

2. Remove corn husks from water and wrap in a towel to keep them from drying.

3. Tear one piece of corn husk lengthwise to a width of about 1$^1/_4$". Tie corn husk in the center with thread. Cup out corn husk on each side.

4. Insert heavy floral wire into styrofoam ball and place styrofoam ball into corn husk "cup" to form the head. Fold remaining end of corn husk down over styrofoam ball until it is completely covered and twist at bottom to form doll's neck. Tie off with thread. Cover the thread with a thin strip of corn husk hot-glued around the neck.

Doll's Arms & Sleeves

5. Roll another piece of corn husk around 11" length of floral wire until corn husk is about $^1/_4$" in diameter. Tie off $^3/_4$" at each end to form doll's hands. Tie off in center with thread.

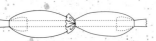

6. Gather wide corn husk around doll's wrist and over doll's hands. Tie off with thread. Turn corn husk back over doll's hands and tie off in center with thread. If corn husks begin to dry, mist with water.

Doll's Chest

7. Lift up end pieces from doll's head and place doll's arm pieces under corn husks. Tie off under arms with thread.

8. Begin to form doll's chest by draping 1$^1/_2$" strips over doll's shoulders, criss-crossing each piece. Repeat process two to three times. Tie off with thread to form doll's waist.

Doll's Skirt

9. Place 10 of the widest corn husks around doll's waist. Gather pieces with wider ends laying over doll's head and sleeves. Tie off tightly with thread. Fold down corn husks, one at a time, to form doll's skirt. Tie down with thread until corn husks dry.

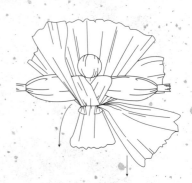

10. Trim skirt to 6$^1/_2$" with scissors.

Doll's Hair

11. Using hot glue gun and glue sticks, hot-glue wool doll hair in place on top center of doll's head, leaving bangs in front. If necessary, fluff doll's hair.

12. Hot-glue straw hat in place on doll's head.

Doll's Shawl

13. Cut fabric into a 7" square with scissors. Fray edges of fabric.

14. Fold fabric square diagonally and place on doll's shoulders.

15. Using hot glue gun and glue sticks, hot-glue shawl under doll's arms to secure.

16. Hot-glue desired accessories into doll's hands.

Corn Husk Wreath

Materials

- Corn husks, dried
- Chile peppers, dried
- Garlic bulbs
- Safflowers, dried
- Caspia
- Statice sinuata
- Lemon leaves, dried
- Grapevine wreath: 4"-diameter
- Raffia
- Fishing line
- Hot glue gun & glue sticks
- Scissors

Instructions

1. Tie corn husks around grapevine wreath with fishing line.

2. Using hot glue gun and glue sticks, hot-glue garlic bulbs, evenly, around wreath.

3. Carefully arrange and hot-glue chile peppers and lemon leaves between garlic bulbs.

4. Carefully arrange and hot-glue safflowers, caspia, and statice sinuata around wreath.

5. Braid several strands of raffia. Thread braid

through bottom of wreath, double, and tie a knot at end.

6. Trim ends of raffia with scissors.

7. Tie raffia in a bow.

8. Using hot glue gun and glue sticks, hot-glue bow at

bottom of raffia braid just above knot.

9. Hot-glue two chile peppers on top of raffia bow.

Corn Husk & Pinecone Santa

Materials

- ❦ Corn husks, dried
- ❦ Pinecones: tiny (8); medium (6); large (1)
- ❦ Acorn hull
- ❦ Wild grass, dried
- ❦ Mustard seeds
- ❦ Cinnamon stick: 5"-long
- ❦ Deer moss
- ❦ Oregon moss
- ❦ Spanish moss
- ❦ Grapevine wreath: 3"-diameter
- ❦ Driftwood
- ❦ Log slab
- ❦ Ground cinnamon: 1 cup
- ❦ Ground cloves: 1 tablespoon
- ❦ Ground nutmeg: 1 tablespoon
- ❦ Applesauce: ³/₄ cup
- ❦ All-purpose glue: 2 tablespoons
- ❦ Water: ³/₄ to 1 cup
- ❦ Styrofoam ball: 1¹/₂"-diameter
- ❦ Wool doll hair
- ❦ Leather scraps
- ❦ Powder blush
- ❦ Raffia
- ❦ Jute, waxed
- ❦ Toothpick
- ❦ Craft glue
- ❦ Hot glue gun & glue sticks
- ❦ Cookie cutter, star-shaped
- ❦ Mixing bowl
- ❦ Wooden spoon
- ❦ Cookie sheet
- ❦ Drill with ³/₈" drill bit
- ❦ Scissors

Instructions

1. Make star-shaped spiced ornaments according to instructions for Making Spiced Ornaments on page 15.

Santa's Body

2. Drill a hole in top of log slab, just off-center, with drill and ³/₈" drill bit.

3. Using hot glue gun and glue sticks, hot-glue cinnamon stick into drilled hole.

4. Hot-glue one large pinecone to top of cinnamon stick for Santa's torso and two medium pinecones to sides of cinnamon stick for Santa's legs.

5. Hot-glue two medium pinecones to sides of large pinecone "torso" for Santa's upper arms and the two remaining medium pinecones, at an angle, to bottom of "upper arms" for Santa's lower arms. Make certain to leave enough space in between to place objects in Santa's lower arms.

6. Apply craft glue to top of log slab and glue Spanish moss on it until it is completely covered. Make certain Santa's legs go down into Spanish moss.

7. Allow glue to dry thoroughly.

Santa's Body

8. Twist one piece of corn husk in the center and place over styrofoam ball. Twist another piece of corn husk in the center and place over styrofoam ball. Wrap corn husks tightly around styrofoam ball.

9. Twist ends of corn husks together at the bottom to form Santa's neck. Tie off with raffia. Trim neck to about ¹/₂" with scissors.

10. Using hot glue gun and glue sticks, hot-glue Santa's head to top of large pinecone "body."

11. Hot-glue wool doll hair in place on top center of Santa's head·and in front for Santa's beard. If necessary, fluff Santa's hair and beard.

12. Hot-glue driftwood inside one of Santa's arms.

13. Hot-glue deer moss to top of driftwood. Hot-glue acorn hull on top of deer moss and hot-glue Oregon moss to front of acorn hull. Hot-glue three tiny pinecones to front of acorn hull.

14. Brush Santa's cheeks with powder blush.

15. Braid several strands of raffia and tie knots at each end.

16. Tie raffia braid around Santa's waist.

17. Fray ends of raffia.

Continued on page 100.

Dried Corn Ornament

Materials

- Corn on cob, dried
- Chile peppers, dried
- Bay leaves, dried
- Cinnamon sticks: 3"-long (2)
- Raffia
- Copper wire: 19-gauge
- Drill with $1/8$" drill bit

Instructions

1. Drill one hole through center of one cinnamon stick with drill and $1/8$" drill bit.

2. Drill two holes through remaining cinnamon stick about $1/2$" apart with drill and $1/8$" drill bit.

3. Thread copper wire through hole in cinnamon stick with one hole. Twist copper wire together to secure.

4. Carefully thread about 12 bay leaves, corn on cob, chile peppers, and about 12 more bay leaves onto copper wire.

5. Thread copper wire through holes in remaining cinnamon stick, leaving a loop for hanging. Twist copper wire together to secure.

6. Tie raffia around copper wire at top of ornament.

Continued from page 99.

Santa's Bag

18. Cut leather in a triangle with scissors. Fold leather down 1" along the side. Bring down remaining two sides to form a "cone" to make Santa's quiver.

19. Overlap the sides and, using a hot glue gun and glue sticks, hot-glue the opening shut.

20. Hot-glue Santa's bag inside Santa's arm opposite the driftwood.

21. Apply craft glue to centers of star-shaped spiced ornaments and glue mustard seeds on them.

22. Allow glue to dry thoroughly.

23. String star-shaped spiced ornaments onto jute so they hang nicely.

24. Using hot glue gun and glue sticks, hot-glue spiced ornaments to side of Santa's bag and hot-glue wild grass inside Santa's bag.

Santa's Hat

25. Cut leather in a $4^1/2$" x 6" triangle with scissors. Wrap leather triangle around back of Santa's head and hot-glue in place.

26. Unwind 3"-diameter grapevine wreath and wrap around Santa's head, then off to one side, and finally around Santa's legs.

27. Using hot glue gun and glue sticks, randomly hot-glue remaining tiny pinecones to grapevine.

Dried Artichoke Wreath

Materials

- Grapevine wreath
- Artichokes, dried
- Sunflower seed head, dried
- Safflowers, dried
- Yarrow, dried
- Poppy pods, dried
- Lemon leaves, dried
- Red leaves, dried
- Twigs
- Cinnamon sticks: 12"-long
- Raffia
- Hot glue gun & glue sticks

Instructions

1. Using hot glue gun and glue sticks, carefully arrange and hot-glue artichokes, sunflower seed head, safflowers, yarrow, poppy pods, lemon leaves, and red leaves around outer edge of wreath. Leave a small section at either side of wreath without drieds.

2. Gather cinnamon sticks and tie raffia around center to secure bundle.

3. Tie raffia in a bow.

4. Using hot glue gun and glue sticks, hot-glue bow to top of cinnamon stick bundle and hot-glue cinnamon stick bundle to top of wreath.

5. Randomly insert twigs around wreath.

Fresh Vegetable Table Centerpiece

Materials

- Tomato candles (3)
- Green leaf lettuce
- Red leaf lettuce
- Baby white potatoes, whole
- Green onions: 1 bunch
- Radishes: 2 bunches

Instructions

1. Wash fresh vegetables and let drain. Pat dry.

2. On the appropriate area of the table, form a circle with green leaf and red leaf lettuce leaves, overlapping as desired, until all lettuce leaves have been used.

3. Embellish centerpiece with baby white potatoes, green onions, and radishes.

4. Place tomato (or other vegetable) candles in center of centerpiece. *Note: This centerpiece will stay fresh for no longer than half a day; it is recommended that this centerpiece be assembled 15 to 30 minutes prior to dinner.*

Fresh Vegetable Napkin Ring

Materials

❦ Radishes
❦ Napkins
❦ Napkin rings

Instructions

1. Wash radishes and pat dry.

2. Fold napkins and place napkin rings in place.

3. Place napkins in center of plates.

4. Embellish napkin rings by placing at least two radishes on the center of each one.

Wild Grass Hanging Spray

Materials

- Wild grass, dried
- Poppy pod, dried
- Thistle blossom, dried
- Safflower, dried
- Tree pod, dried
- Nigella, dried
- Pinecone
- Jute: 4-ply
- Copper wire: 19-gauge
- Hot glue gun & glue sticks

Instructions

1. Fold jute in half. Tie a knot about 3" down from center to make a loop for hanging.

2. Gather wild grass into three bundles and tie copper wire around center of each bundle to secure.

3. Tie one wild grass bundle with jute just below knot and tie a knot to secure. Repeat process for two remaining wild grass bundles.

4. Randomly tie knots in tails.

5. Using hot glue gun and glue sticks, hot-glue the poppy pod and the thistle blossom to the center of the first wild grass bundle.

6. Hot-glue the safflower and the tree pod to the center of the second wild grass bundle.

7. Hot-glue the nigella and the pinecone to the center of the third wild grass bundle.

8. When wild grass hanging spray gets too dusty to clean, it can be used as a firestarter.

Twigs & Branches ...

Bird's Nest Wreath

Photograph on page 105.

Materials

- Spanish moss
- Leaves, dried
- Twigs
- Caspia
- Poppy pods, dried
- Wooden egg
- Acrylic paints
- Paintbrush
- Toothbrush
- Foam plate
- Acrylic spray, gloss
- Acrylic spray, matte
- Adhesive spray
- Floral wire
- Craft glue
- Hot glue gun & glue sticks

Instructions

1. Paint wooden egg according to instructions for Painting Wooden Eggs on page 13.

2. Make bird's nest according to instructions for Making Bird Nests on page 12.

3. Using twigs, form a circle. Intertwine several twigs to hold formed circle. Wire with floral wire to secure.

4. Apply craft glue to bottom of bird's nest and glue to bottom of circle.

5. Allow glue to dry thoroughly.

6. Using hot glue gun and glue sticks, hot-glue caspia to each side of bird's nest.

7. Hot-glue poppy pods to each side of bird's nest.

8. Hot-glue wooden egg into bird's nest.

Wasp's Nest Wooden Bowl

Materials

- Wooden bowl, heart-shaped
- Leaves, dried
- Mushrooms, dried
- Deer moss
- Birch twigs
- Copper wire: 19-gauge
- Styrofoam egg: small
- Toilet paper, white
- Acrylic paints:
  Dark gray
  Light gray
- Paintbrush
- Spray bottle
- Craft knife
- Pencil
- Craft glue
- Hot glue gun & glue sticks

Instructions

1. Make wasp's nest according to instructions for Making Wasp Nests on page 12.

2. Using twigs, form a circle. Intertwine several twigs to hold formed circle. Wire with copper wire to secure.

3. Apply craft glue to back of wasp's nest and glue to side of twig wreath.

4. Allow glue to dry thoroughly.

5. Using hot glue gun and glue sticks, hot-glue twig wreath inside wooden bowl.

6. Hot-glue leaves, mushrooms, and deer moss around twig wreath.

Aspen Log Table Spray

Materials

- Aspen logs: 1"-diameter, 10"-long (5)
- Pomegranates, dried
- Pinecones
- Whole nutmeg
- Cinnamon sticks
- Jute: 2-ply
- Raffia
- Craft glue

Instructions

1. Gather logs and tie jute around center to secure bundle.

2. Cover jute with raffia.

3. Tie raffia in a bow.

4. Apply craft glue to pomegranates, pinecones, whole nutmeg, and cinnamon sticks.

5. Carefully arrange pomegranates, pinecones, whole nutmeg, and cinnamon sticks on top of raffia bow.

6. Allow glue to dry thoroughly.

Knot-Hole Photo Frame

Materials

- Photograph: to fit opening
- Log with knot
- Copper wire: 19-gauge
- Saw
- Hammer
- Nail
- Stapler & staples

Instructions

1. Slice back off log with saw so it is flat.

2. If the knot is still in the log, carefully remove it to leave a hole in the log.

3. Form a copper wire loop and nail to back side of log for hanging.

4. Using a stapler, carefully staple photograph to back side of log.

Aspen & Pussy Willow Birdhouse

Materials

- Aspen log:
  5"-high x
  2"-diameter
- Cedar slat:
  2¼"-wide x
  5"-long x
  ¼"-thick
- Wooden dowels:
  ⅜"-diameter,
  8"-long;
  ⅜"-diameter,
  1"-long
- Clay pot:
  4"-diameter
- Styrofoam ball:
  3"-diameter
- Oregon moss
- Deer moss
- Pussy willows
- Willow twigs
- Wired ribbon,
  ¾"-wide,
  purple-blue
  ombré
- Floral wire
- Craft glue
- Hot glue gun &
  glue sticks
- Wood glue
- Saw
- Drill with
  ⅜" & ¾"
  drill bits
- Scissors

Instructions

1. Cut top of log at an angle with saw.

2. Drill a hole in bottom center of log with drill and ⅜" drill bit.

3. Drill a hole, 1"-deep, in front center of log with drill and ¾" drill bit.

4. Drill a hole in front center of log, just below ¾" hole, with drill and ⅜" drill bit.

5. Using wood glue, adhere cedar slat to top of log to make birdhouse roof.

6. Fill ⅜" holes with wood glue and insert 8" wooden dowel in hole in bottom center of log to make a stand and insert 1" wooden dowel in hole in front center of log to make a perch.

7. Allow glue to dry thoroughly.

8. Using hot glue gun and glue sticks, hot-glue styrofoam ball into clay pot.

9. Push 8" wooden dowel with log birdhouse attached into center of styrofoam ball.

10. Push pussy willows and twigs into styrofoam ball around log birdhouse.

11. Apply craft glue to styrofoam ball and glue Oregon moss around it until it is completely covered.

12. Apply craft glue to top of Oregon moss and glue deer moss on it, covering the wooden dowel.

13. Apply craft glue around cedar slat and glue Oregon moss around it.

14. Allow glue to dry thoroughly.

15. Tie wired ribbon in a bow according to instructions for Making Multi-Loop Bows on page 14.

16. Using hot glue gun and glue sticks, hot-glue bow to a willow twig. Cascade ribbon tails down and hot-glue in place.

Grapevine Wreath Basket

Materials

- Grapevine wreaths: 10"-diameter; 3"-diameter
- Twigs
- Branch, green
- Pomegranates, dried
- Acorns
- Sunflower seed heads, dried
- Poppy pods, dried
- Mushrooms, dried
- Star anise, dried
- Cinnamon sticks
- Pinecones
- Tree bark
- Deer moss
- Clay pot: 1¹/₂"-diameter
- Copper wire: 19-gauge
- Saw
- Hot glue gun & glue sticks

Instructions

1. Cut twigs with saw to fit inside diameter of 10" grapevine wreath.

2. Criss-cross twigs, hooking them into sides of grapevine wreath.

3. Bend green branch into the shape of a handle and secure it on opposite sides of grapevine wreath with copper wire.

4. Allow basket to sit in the sun for several days for green branch to dry thoroughly.

5. Using hot glue gun and glue sticks, carefully arrange and hot-glue pomegranates, acorns, sunflower seed heads, poppy pods, mushrooms, star anise, cinnamon sticks, pinecones, tree bark, and deer moss around outside edges of grapevine wreath.

6. Hot-glue clay pot to top of arrangement and hot-glue deer moss inside.

7. Intertwine several twigs around basket's handle.

8. Unwind 3"-diameter grapevine wreath and wrap around basket's handle.

Grapevine Birdhouse

Materials

- Birdhouse on base
- Grapevine wreath
- Yarrow, dried
- Spanish moss
- Craft glue
- Hot glue gun & glue sticks

Instructions

1. Unwind grapevine wreath and wrap around birdhouse.

2. Apply craft glue to base of birdhouse and glue Spanish moss around it until it is completely covered.

3. Allow glue to dry thoroughly.

4. Using hot glue gun and glue sticks, hot-glue yarrow around base of birdhouse on top of Spanish moss and to grapevine around roof of birdhouse.

Twig Topiary

Materials

- ❧ Twigs, green
- ❧ Branches: 10" (3)
- ❧ Spanish moss
- ❧ Raffia
- ❧ Clay pot with saucer: 3¹/₂"-diameter
- ❧ Styrofoam ball: 3"-diameter
- ❧ String
- ❧ Craft glue
- ❧ Hot glue gun & glue sticks
- ❧ Scissors

Instructions

1. Using hot glue gun and glue sticks, hot-glue styrofoam ball into clay pot.

2. Hot-glue clay pot to saucer.

3. Push 10" branches into center of styrofoam ball.

4. Apply craft glue to styrofoam ball and glue Spanish moss around it until it is completely covered.

5. Allow glue to dry thoroughly.

6. Begin wrapping green twigs around top of branches until a 4"-diameter ball is formed.

7. Wrap the formed "twig ball" with string to secure.

8. Allow topiary to sit in the sun for several days for green twigs to dry thoroughly.

9. Carefully remove string from topiary.

10. Tie raffia around branches.

11. Trim ends of raffia with scissors.

Log Wreath

Materials

- Logs:
  1"-diameter,
  3"-long (6)
- Cedar roses
- Poppy pods, dried
- Cockscomb,
  dried
- Deer moss
- Copper wire:
  19-gauge
- Hot glue gun &
  glue sticks
- Wood glue
- Saw
- Hammer
- Nails

Instructions

1. Cut both ends of each log at an angle with saw.

2. Apply wood glue to end of each log and, using a hammer, carefully nail logs together to form a hexagon.

3. Allow glue to dry thoroughly.

4. Form a copper wire loop and nail to back side of log wreath for hanging.

5. Using a hot glue gun and glue sticks, hot-glue deer moss to bottom front of log wreath.

6. Carefully arrange and hot-glue cedar roses, poppy pods, and cockscomb on top of deer moss.

7. If desired, turn this log wreath into a log photo frame by carefully stapling a photograph to the back side of log wreath.

Star Anise Wreath

Materials

- Grapevine wreath
- Star anise, dried
- Cinnamon sticks
- Baby's breath,
  dried
- Copper wire:
  19-gauge
- Wired ribbon,
  ³/₄"-wide,
  green-white
  ombré
- Floral wire
- Hot glue gun &
  glue sticks
- Scissors

Instructions

1. Break cinnamon sticks into uniform lengths.

2. Using hot glue gun and glue sticks, hot-glue star anise around grapevine wreath until it is completely covered.

3. Hot-glue cinnamon sticks at top of wreath on top of star anise.

4. Hot-glue baby's breath into wreath around cinnamon sticks.

5. Tie wired ribbon in a bow according to instructions for Making Multi-Loop Bows on page 14.

6. Using hot glue gun and glue sticks, hot-glue bow to top of wreath in center of cinnamon stick arrangement. Cascade ribbon tails down.

7. Thread copper wire through grapevine wreath for hanging.

Grapevine & Tree Bark Birdhouse with Wild Grass

Materials

- Grapevine wreath
- Tree bark (3 pieces)
- Wild grass, dried
- Poppy pods, dried
- Oregon moss
- Jute: 2-ply
- Copper wire: 19-gauge
- Hot glue gun & glue sticks
- Drill with 1/8" drill bit
- Scissors

Instructions

1. Drill two holes through center of each piece of tree bark about 1/2" apart with drill and 1/8" drill bit.

2. Thread copper wire through holes on tree bark and wire in place around grapevine wreath to form a roof for the birdhouse. Wire the third piece of tree bark to the bottom of the grapevine wreath to form a base for the birdhouse. Twist copper wires to secure.

3. Cut jute with scissors and thread through where tree bark meets to form roof and tie a knot to make a loop for hanging.

4. Gather wild grass and poppy pods and tie jute around center to secure bundle.

5. Using hot glue gun and glue sticks, hot-glue Oregon moss to roof of birdhouse.

6. Hot-glue wild grass bundle to roof of birdhouse on top of Oregon moss.

7. Tie jute in a bow and hot-glue to center of bundle.

Grapevine & Tree Bark Birdhouse with Lantern Pods

Materials

- Grapevine wreath
- Tree bark (3 pieces)
- Twigs
- Lantern pods, dried
- Raffia
- Copper wire: 19-gauge
- Hot glue gun & glue sticks
- Drill with $1/8$" drill bit

Instructions

1. Drill two holes through center of each piece of tree bark about $1/2$" apart with drill and $1/8$" drill bit.

2. Thread copper wire through holes on tree bark and

wire in place around grapevine wreath to form a roof for the birdhouse. Wire the third piece of tree bark to the bottom of the grapevine

wreath. Twist copper wires to secure.

3. Gather twigs and lantern pods and tie raffia around center to secure bundle.

4. Using hot glue gun and glue sticks, hot-glue bundle to tree bark at bottom of grapevine wreath.

5. Tie raffia in a bow and hot-glue to center of bundle.

Picket Fence Wreath

Materials

- Wooden picket fence
- Spanish moss
- Leaves, dried
- Twigs
- Juniper berries, dried
- Red leaves, dried
- Oregon moss
- Acorns
- Curly willow wreath: 8" diameter
- Wooden egg
- Acrylic paints
- Paintbrush
- Toothbrush
- Foam plate
- Acrylic spray, gloss
- Acrylic spray, matte
- Adhesive spray
- Craft glue
- Hot glue gun & glue sticks

Instructions

1. Paint wooden egg according to instructions for Painting Wooden Eggs on page 13.

2. Make bird's nest according to instructions for Making Bird Nests on page 12.

3. Using a paintbrush, paint wooden picket fence with acrylic paint.

4. Allow paint to dry thoroughly.

5. Using a toothbrush, spatter wooden picket fence with acrylic paint.

6. Allow paint to dry thoroughly.

7. Apply craft glue to bottom of bird's nest and glue to one side of wooden picket fence.

8. Allow glue to dry thoroughly.

9. Using hot glue gun and glue sticks, carefully arrange and hot-glue red leaves around bird's nest.

10. Carefully arrange and hot-glue juniper berries and acorns around bird's nest.

11. Randomly place small amounts of Oregon moss around acorns on top of bird's nest.

12. Intertwine several twigs around bird's nest.

13. Using hot glue gun and glue sticks, hot-glue wooden egg into bird's nest.

Birch Birdhouse

Materials

- Birch log: 4³/₄"-high x 3"-diameter
- Birch log slab: 5"-diameter
- Cedar slats: 3¹/₂"-square x ¹/₄"-thick (2)
- Wooden dowel: ¹/₄"-diameter, 1"-long
- Wood glue
- Saw
- Hammer
- Nails
- Drill with ⁷/₈" & ¹/₄" drill bits

Instructions

1. Cut top of birch log at angles with saw to form desired roof pitch.

2. Drill one ⁷/₈"-hole 1¹/₂" down from top of log with drill and ⁷/₈" drill bit.

3. Drill one ¹/₄"-hole 3" down from top of log with drill and ¹/₄" drill bit.

4. Using wood glue, glue wooden dowel into ¹/₄" hole to make a perch.

5. Glue log to log slab and glue cedar slats on top of log to make a roof.

6. Allow glue to dry thoroughly.

7. Using a hammer, nail log to log slab and nail cedar slats to roof to secure.

Metal Heart Hanger

Materials

- Sheet metal
- Branch
- Grapevine wreath: 4"-diameter
- Steel wire, 19-gauge
- Saucepan
- Vinegar: 1 cup
- Salt: $^1/_2$ cup
- Water: $^1/_2$ cup
- Tin snips
- Drill with $^1/_8$" drill bit

Instructions

1. Cut and oxidize three sheet metal hearts according to instructions for Cutting and Oxidizing Metal on page 14.

2. Drill a hole in the top center of each heart with drill and $^1/_8$" drill bit.

3. Wrap steel wire around each end of branch to make a handle for hanging.

4. Thread steel wire through drilled hole in each heart. Twist in back of heart to secure, leaving four-inch long tail.

5. Wrap tails around branch two to three times.

6. Unwind grapevine wreath and wrap around branch.

Log Candelabra

Materials

- Logs:
  2¹⁄₂"-diameter,
  12¹⁄₂"-long;
  ³⁄₄"-diameter,
  6"-long (4);
  ¹⁄₂"-diameter,
  8"-long (4)
- Pinecones
- Pine boughs
- Jute: 3-ply
- Metal
  candle cups:
  to fit diameter
  of candle (4)
- Tapered
  candles (4)
- Acrylic paint:
  White
- Paintbrush
- Hot glue gun &
  glue sticks
- Wood glue
- Flat screws,
  1¹⁄₂" (4)
- Craft knife
- Saw
- Drill with
  ³⁄₄" drill bit

Instructions

1. Slice 12¹⁄₂"-long log in half lengthwise with saw and cut log halves into the shapes shown in diagram at right.

2. Drill one ³⁄₄" hole at each end of both log halves, 1" from each end.

3. Using wood glue, glue base together. Next, glue 6"-long logs into drilled holes. If necessary, whittle logs with a craft knife for a perfect fit.

4. Allow glue to dry thoroughly.

5. Using flat screws, attach one metal candle cup to top of each 6"-long (upright) log.

6. Using hot glue gun and glue sticks, hot-glue 8"-long logs around tops of 6"-long (upright) logs. Wrap jute around each corner and tuck ends under to secure.

7. Using hot glue gun and glue sticks, hot-glue pinecones and pine boughs on top of base.

8. Using a paintbrush, randomly dab white acrylic paint over pinecones.

9. Allow paint to dry thoroughly.

10. Carefully place candles in metal candle cups.

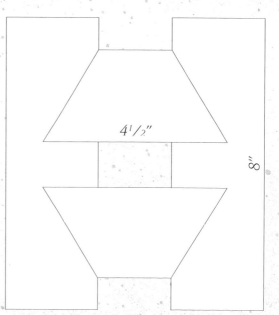

4¹⁄₂"

8"

Barnwood Birdhouse

Materials

- Barnwood with knot
- Tree bark
- Spanish moss
- Leaves, dried
- Twigs
- Wooden egg
- Acrylic paints
- Paintbrush
- Toothbrush
- Foam plate
- Steel wire, 19-gauge
- Acrylic spray, gloss
- Acrylic spray, matte
- Adhesive spray
- Craft glue
- Hot glue gun & glue sticks
- Wood glue
- Pencil
- Hammer
- Nails

Instructions

1. Paint wooden egg according to instructions for Painting Wooden Eggs on page 13.

2. Make bird's nest according to instructions for Making Bird Nests on page 12.

3. If the knot is still in the barnwood, carefully remove it to leave a hole in the barnwood.

4. Using a hammer, drive one nail into each side of barnwood.

5. Wrap steel wire around a pencil to curl and wrap steel wire around each nail to make a handle for hanging.

6. Using wood glue, adhere tree bark across top of barnwood.

7. Allow glue to dry thoroughly.

8. Apply craft glue to bottom of bird's nest and glue inside knot in barnwood.

9. Allow glue to dry thoroughly.

10. Using hot glue gun and glue sticks, hot-glue wooden egg into bird's nest.

Soaps ...

Stacked Bars of Soap Embellished with Wheat Stem & Cinnamon Stick

Photograph on page 121.

Materials

❧ Bars of natural soap, round (3)
❧ Wheat stem, dried
❧ Pinecones
❧ Cinnamon stick
❧ Jute: 3-ply
❧ Hot glue gun & glue sticks

Instructions

1. Make bars of natural soap according to instructions for Making Natural Soap on page 16.

2. Stack three bars of soap on top of each other.

3. Tie jute around bars of soap twice in each direction.

4. Tie jute in a bow on top of stacked soap.

5. Using hot glue gun and glue sticks, hot-glue wheat, pinecones, and cinnamon stick on top of jute bow.

Wrapped Bar of Soap Embellished with a Raffia Braid & Cinnamon Stick

Photograph on page 121.

Materials

❧ Bar of natural soap
❧ Cinnamon stick
❧ Raffia
❧ Natural paper
❧ Cellophane tape
❧ Hot glue gun & glue sticks

Instructions

1. Make bar of natural soap according to instructions for Making Natural Soap on page 16.

2. Wrap natural paper around bar of soap. Secure with cellophane tape.

3. Braid several strands of raffia and tie knots at each end.

4. Tie raffia braid around bar of soap.

5. Fray ends of raffia.

6. Insert cinnamon stick into raffia braid knot.

Stacked Bars of Soap Embellished with Licopodium & Cinnamon Sticks

Photograph on page 121.

Materials

❧ Bars of natural soap (3)
❧ Licopodium
❧ Cinnamon sticks
❧ Jute: 3-ply
❧ Corrugated paper: 1"-wide
❧ Cellophane tape
❧ Hot glue gun & glue sticks

Instructions

1. Make bars of natural soap according to instructions for Making Natural Soap on page 16.

2. Stack three bars of soap on top of each other.

3. Wrap corrugated paper around bars of soap. Secure with cellophane tape.

4. Using hot glue gun and glue sticks, hot-glue licopodium and cinnamon sticks on top of corrugated paper.

5. Tie jute around bars of soap once in each direction.

6. Tie jute in a bow at top of stacked soap.

Bars of Soap Embellished with Bay Leaves or Orange Slices

Photograph on page 121.

Materials

❧ Bars of natural soap
❧ Bay leaves, dried
❧ Orange slices, dried
❧ Raffia
❧ Natural paper
❧ Corrugated paper: 1"-wide, optional
❧ Cellophane tape
❧ Hot glue gun & glue sticks

Instructions

1. Make bars of natural soap according to instructions for Making Natural Soap on page 16.

2. Wrap natural paper around bars of soap. Secure with cellophane tape.

Continued on page 123.

Bars of Soap Embellished with Pressed Flowers & Greenery

Materials

- Bars of natural soap, round
- Pressed flowers
- Pressed greenery
- Tweezers
- Toothpick
- Craft glue
- Découpage glue
- Paintbrush

Instructions

1. Make bars of natural soap according to instructions for Making Natural Soap on page 16.

2. Using tweezers, pick up pressed flowers and greenery.

3. Using a toothpick, apply craft glue to back sides of pressed flowers and greenery.

4. Carefully arrange pressed flowers and greenery on top of bars of soap.

5. Allow glue to dry thoroughly.

6. Using a paintbrush, apply découpage glue over pressed flowers and greenery on top of bars of soap according to manufacturer's directions.

Continued from page 122.

Continued from page 122.

3. If desired, wrap corrugated paper around bars of soap. Secure with cellophane tape.

4. Using hot glue gun and glue sticks, hot-glue bay leaves or orange slices on top of natural or corrugated papers.

5. Tie raffia around bars of soap once in each direction.

6. Tie raffia in a bow on top of soap.

Loofah Embellished with Licopodium & Cinnamon Sticks

Materials

- Loofah
- Licopodium
- Cinnamon sticks
- Star anise, dried
- Raffia
- Natural paper
- Corrugated paper: 1"-wide
- Cellophane tape
- Hot glue gun & glue sticks

Instructions

1. Peel loofah and allow to dry completely.

2. Wrap natural paper around loofah. Secure with cellophane tape.

3. Wrap corrugated paper around loofah. Secure with cellophane tape.

4. Using hot glue gun and glue sticks, hot-glue licopodium, cinnamon sticks, and star anise on top of corrugated paper.

5. Tie raffia around loofah.

6. Tie raffia in a bow on top of loofah.

Loofah Embellished with River Birch Twigs & Cones

Materials

- Loofah
- River birch twigs
- River birch cones
- Raffia
- Natural paper
- Corrugated paper: 1"-wide
- Cellophane tape
- Hot gluc gun & glue sticks

Instructions

1. Peel loofah and allow to dry completely.

2. Wrap natural paper around loofah. Secure with cellophane tape.

3. Wrap corrugated paper around loofah. Secure with cellophane tape.

4. Using hot glue gun and glue sticks, hot-glue river birch twigs and cones on top of corrugated paper.

5. Tie raffia around loofah.

6. Tie raffia in a bow on top of loofah.

Stacked Bars of Soap Embellished with Wild Grass & Foxtail Millet

Materials

- Bars of natural soap, round (2)
- Wild grass, dried
- Foxtail millet, dried
- Jute: 3-ply
- Hot glue gun & glue sticks

Instructions

1. Make bars of natural soap according to instructions for Making Natural Soap on page 16.

2. Stack two bars of soap on top of each other.

3. Tie jute around bars of soap once in each direction.

4. Tie jute in a bow on top of stacked soap.

5. Using hot glue gun and glue sticks, hot-glue wild grass and foxtail millet on top of jute bow.

Metric Conversions ...

INCHES TO MILLIMETRES AND CENTIMETRES

MM-Millimetres CM-Centimetres

INCHES	MM	CM	INCHES	CM	INCHES	CM
$1/8$	3	0.9	9	22.9	30	76.2
$1/4$	6	0.6	10	25.4	31	78.7
$3/8$	10	1.0	11	27.9	32	81.3
$1/2$	13	1.3	12	30.5	33	83.8
$5/8$	16	1.6	13	33.0	34	86.4
$3/4$	19	1.9	14	35.6	35	88.9
$7/8$	22	2.2	15	38.1	36	91.4
1	25	2.5	16	40.6	37	94.0
$1 1/4$	32	3.2	17	43.2	38	96.5
$1 1/2$	38	3.8	18	45.7	39	99.1
$1 3/4$	44	4.4	19	48.3	40	101.6
2	51	5.1	20	50.8	41	104.1
$2 1/2$	64	6.4	21	53.3	42	106.7
3	76	7.6	22	55.9	43	109.2
$3 1/2$	89	8.9	23	58.4	44	111.8
4	102	10.2	24	61.0	45	114.3
$4 1/2$	114	11.4	25	63.5	46	116.8
5	127	12.7	26	66.0	47	119.4
6	152	15.2	27	68.6	48	121.9
7	178	17.8	28	71.1	49	124.5
8	203	20.3	29	73.7	50	127.0

YARDS TO METRES

YARDS	METRES	YARDS	METRES	YARDS	METRES	YARDS	METRES	YARDS	METRES
$1/8$	0.11	$2 1/8$	1.94	$4 1/8$	3.77	$6 1/8$	5.60	$8 1/8$	7.43
$1/4$	0.23	$2 1/4$	2.06	$4 1/4$	3.89	$6 1/4$	5.72	$8 1/4$	7.54
$3/8$	0.34	$2 3/8$	2.17	$4 3/8$	4.00	$6 3/8$	5.83	$8 3/8$	7.66
$1/2$	0.46	$2 1/2$	2.29	$4 1/2$	4.11	$6 1/2$	5.94	$8 1/2$	7.77
$5/8$	0.57	$2 5/8$	2.40	$4 5/8$	4.23	$6 5/8$	6.06	$8 5/8$	7.89
$3/4$	0.69	$2 3/4$	2.51	$4 3/4$	4.34	$6 3/4$	6.17	$8 3/4$	8.00
$7/8$	0.80	$2 7/8$	2.63	$4 7/8$	4.46	$6 7/8$	6.29	$8 7/8$	8.12
1	0.91	3	2.74	5	4.57	7	6.40	9	8.23
$1 1/8$	1.03	$3 1/8$	2.86	$5 1/8$	4.69	$7 1/8$	6.52	$9 1/8$	8.34
$1 1/4$	1.14	$3 1/4$	2.97	$5 1/4$	4.80	$7 1/4$	6.63	$9 1/4$	8.46
$1 3/8$	1.26	$3 3/8$	3.09	$5 3/8$	4.91	$7 3/8$	6.74	$9 3/8$	8.57
$1 1/2$	1.37	$3 1/2$	3.20	$5 1/2$	5.03	$7 1/2$	6.86	$9 1/2$	8.69
$1 5/8$	1.49	$3 5/8$	3.31	$5 5/8$	5.14	$7 5/8$	6.97	$9 5/8$	8.80
$1 3/4$	1.60	$3 3/4$	3.43	$5 3/4$	5.26	$7 3/4$	7.09	$9 3/4$	8.92
$1 7/8$	1.71	$3 7/8$	3.54	$5 7/8$	5.37	$7 7/8$	7.20	$9 7/8$	9.03
2	1.83	4	3.66	6	5.49	8	7.32	10	9.14

Index ...